Practical, ethical and eff
enforcement today. A
weaponless defense and
techniques for law enforce....
maximum protection to the officer and us..
minimum appropriate force.

**Procedures to avoid and prevent assault.

**Preparation to deal effectively with many
common assault situations without reliance on
firearms.

**Ways of coping with the actual problems the
working police officer encounters on the job.

**Tactics cover a wide range of situations--from
mild resistance to defending against dangerous
assault.

**Unlike traditional martial arts, these tactics
can be learned in a relatively short time.

This book is intended for professionals in law
enforcement and security work, for academy
programs and for police science and adminis-
tration of justice courses at the college level.

REVIEW EXCERPTS

"...*Defense Tactics*... by Bruce Tegner, a noted authority
in the field ... would be an excellent textbook for a basic
course in self-defense..." LAW BOOKS IN REVIEW

" ... a practical tool for police academy programs, police
programs at the university level, and for the (individual)
officer ..." THE POLICE CHIEF

BOOKS by BRUCE TEGNER

BRUCE TEGNER'S COMPLETE BOOK of SELF-DEFENSE
SELF-DEFENSE: A BASIC COURSE
SELF-DEFENSE NERVE CENTERS & PRESSURE POINTS
DEFENSE TACTICS for LAW ENFORCEMENT
Weaponless Defense & Control and Baton Techniques
STICK-FIGHTING: SELF-DEFENSE
STICK-FIGHTING: SPORT FORMS
KUNG FU & TAI CHI
SAVATE: FRENCH FOOT & FIST FIGHTING
KARATE & JUDO EXERCISES
BRUCE TEGNER'S COMPLETE BOOK of JUJITSU
JUDO: BEGINNER to BLACK BELT
KARATE: BEGINNER to BLACK BELT
AIKIDO & BOKATA

BOOKS by BRUCE TEGNER & ALICE McGRATH

SELF-DEFENSE & ASSAULT PREVENTION for
    GIRLS & WOMEN
SELF-DEFENSE for YOUR CHILD
Elementary school age boys & girls
SOLO FORMS of KARATE, TAI CHI, AIKIDO
    & KUNG FU

BOOKS by Ellen Kei Hua

KUNG FU MEDITATIONS & Chinese Proverbial Wisdom
MEDITATIONS of the MASTERS

DEFENSE TACTICS for LAW ENFORCEMENT:

WEAPONLESS DEFENSE & CONTROL and BATON TECHNIQUES

BRUCE TEGNER

THOR PUBLISHING COMPANY
VENTURA CA 93002

Library of Congress Cataloging in Publication Data

Tegner, Bruce.
    Defense tactics for law enforcement: weaponless defense & control and baton techniques.

    Includes index.
    CONTENTS: Weaponless defense & control; baton techniques
    1. Arrest (Police methods) 2. Self-defense 3. Baton techniques
I. Title
HV8080.A6T4   1978   363.2'3   77-28136
ISBN 0-87407-028-7

DEFENSE TACTICS for LAW ENFORCEMENT:
Weaponless Defense & Control and Baton Techniques

THOR PUBLISHING COMPANY
P. O. BOX 1782
VENTURA CA 93002   PRINTED IN U.S.A.

BRUCE TEGNER BOOKS REVIEWED

KARATE: BEGINNER to BLACK BELT
"Techniques and routines...illustrated in profuse detail...
specially geared to a Y.A. audience."
                        KLIATT YOUNG ADULT PB GUIDE

SELF-DEFENSE: A BASIC COURSE
"An eminently practical, concise guide to self-defense...for
young men..."   American Library Association BOOKLIST

"YA - A calm, nonsexist approach to simple yet effective self-
defense techniques...clear photographs...sound advice."
                        SCHOOL LIBRARY JOURNAL

BRUCE TEGNER'S COMPLETE BOOK OF JUJITSU
"...authoritative and easy-to-follow text..."
                        SCHOOL LIBRARY JOURNAL

BRUCE TEGNER'S COMPLETE BOOK OF SELF-DEFENSE
Recommended for Y.A. in the American Library Association
                        BOOKLIST

SELF-DEFENSE & ASSAULT PREVENTION FOR GIRLS & WOMEN (with
Alice McGrath)
"...should be required reading for all girls and women..."
                        WILSON LIBRARY BULLETIN

"...simple and straightforward with no condescension...easy to
learn and viable as defense tactics..."   SCHOOL LIBRARY JOURNAL

SELF-DEFENSE FOR YOUR CHILD (with Alice McGrath)
[For elementary school-age boys & girls]
"...informative, readable book for family use..."
                        CHRISTIAN HOME & SCHOOL

DEFENSE TACTICS FOR LAW ENFORCEMENT
"...an excellent textbook for a basic course in self-defense..."
                        LAW BOOKS IN REVIEW

"...a practical tool for police academy programs, police programs
at the university level, and for the (individual) officer..."
                        THE POLICE CHIEF

SELF-DEFENSE NERVE CENTERS & PRESSURE POINTS
"...a practical guide to the most effective weaponless self-defense
using the least possible force..."   THE POLICE CHIEF

KUNG FU & TAI CHI: Chinese Karate and Classical Exercise
"...recommended for physical fitness collections."
                        LIBRARY JOURNAL

SOLO FORMS of Karate, Tai Chi, Aikido & Kung Fu (with Alice McGrath)
"...well-coordinated, step-by-step instructions...carefully captioned
photos...for personal enjoyment and exercise..." YA
                        American Library Association BOOKLIST

Dedicated to the memory of

LT. HARVEY A. VARAT

Lt. Varat was a member of the Ventura County Sheriff's Department. He helped generously in the preparation of the original version of this book.

Hank Varat was professional, competent, compassionate and concerned. He was loved and respected. His sudden death in 1973 deprived us of an exceptionally good man who was a fine officer.

RICHARD WINDISHAR and LT. HARVEY A. VARAT demonstrate most of the weaponless techniques with the author. Officers RICHARD J. NICKOLOFF and WILLIAM D. ESMAY demonstrate most of the baton techniques. Alice McGrath, Harry Rosemond, Kathy Wilson and Neil Ziegler assisted.

CONTENTS

CONTENTS

BATON TECHNIQUES 143

INTRODUCTION

PEACE-KEEPING IN A VIOLENT AGE

There is abundant evidence of violence in our society. It is there in the crime statistics, in news stories, in magazines, in movies and on television. At the same time, there is an increasing resentment of violence. There are contradictions in the way this resentment is expressed. Some of the public expects the police to control crime without resorting to counter-violence, while some of the public encourages the police to use all possible force to contain the force they fear.

Law enforcement does not exist in a vacuum. The tactics which are used by law enforcement agencies must meet these criteria: They are expected to be effective for achieving control of crime and maintenance of the peace; and they are expected to be consistent with the stated values of the society.

In a repressive society, police work is only required to be efficient; it is not expected to be civilized, humane or ethical. In a repressive society, force is the crucial part of law enforcement-- law offers little protection from force.

In a society which values freedom, the police are expected to behave according to the values of a free society. The officer is expected to demonstrate respect for the individual and demonstrate a sense of fairness. The police officer is supposed to personify *decency*. Clearly, the concept of a civilized officer in a civilized society includes the concept of the least use of force and the maximum protection of law.

PROFESSIONAL STANDARDS

Professions are deemed to exist as professions when there are standards, generally recognized criteria of preparation and education, and well-defined outlines of what the profession is engaged in doing.

The possible range of actions in most police field work is: verbal request or command, management by physical means without weapons, use of the baton, and finally, maximum use of force--the gun.

In the area of work which involves the maximum force, use of the gun, there is regulation and control and there is considerable attention to the preparation of the officer to use that degree of force. First there is training, and then most departments require periodic demonstrations to make certain that the officer is maintaining an appropriate level of skill.

Non-forceful management of police problems is being given increasing attention in academy training, in police science courses and in research.

Professional skill of the highest order is required for managing without force. Verbal command and request, the show of authority, the appearance of being in control, persuasion and mediation are everyday procedures on the job. There are many very good officers who are so skillful at non-forceful management of difficult situations that they rarely need to consider the use of any degree of force.

It is in the area between no force and maximum force that there are no standards and no general agreement. Concerning the subject of weaponless defense and control there is no definition of what constitutes "reasonable" as compared with "needless" force.

In baton training there is a wide range of tactics and techniques and no general agreement about those which are both efficient and acceptable, and no definition of those which are unnecessarily forceful.

NEEDLESS FORCE: A DEFINITION

The use of unnecessary force arises from attitudes of contempt or fear, or it results from inadequate preparation to cope with assault or resistance. When even a small degree of force is applied in a situation where it is not necessary, that is needless use of force.

A skilled officer needs to know weaponless defense in addition to marksmanship and baton techniques in order to have a suitable range of choices. The officer who cannot handle assault without weapons has only the choice between no force or maximum force.

The officer who knows weaponless defense and control tactics is not going to be under the same kind of pressure as the officer who can only choose between no force and maximum force. The officer who has the ability to handle assault without weapons is more likely to be confident, convincing and persuasive--thus diminishing the possibility of having to rely on any force at all.

WHICH TECHNIQUES FOR LEAST FORCE?

Degrees of force cannot be measured merely by describing the
type of tactic being used.

Any specific tactic or group of tactics might be ethical in one
set of circumstances and not in another. All fighting styles
employ some tactics which could be called brutal. This is true
of judo, boxing, karate, wrestling, aikido and jujitsu. Further,
some tactics are brutal if used by one individual and not even
effective when used by others.

A judo throw might be a vicious technique if applied by an
expert, but if it were attempted by someone with moderate
skill, it might be useless. It is not easy to throw a resisting
individual, but if a judo throw were used on the street, instead
of on a mat, the result could be serious injury. To measure the
use of force it is essential to consider the range of possibilities
of result--*to the subject!* Reasonable use of force can only be
evaluated by comparison with available alternatives.

Similarly, an aikido wrist-twist hold would be appropriate in
some situations, useless in others and needless force in some
situations. Against an unresisting individual, a wrist-twist hold
might be unnecessary force; against a resisting individual it
might be ineffective if used by an officer with a moderate degree
of skill; it might be dangerous if used forcefully against a frail
or vulnerable subject.

A kick into the knee would be needless force under some
circumstances, but it is clearly less use of force than using a
gun. Using a kick instead of a gun would be the most ethical
tactic if it would be effective. Kicking a non-resisting or vulnerable subject is clearly needless use of force.

The use of a gun when a violent individual can be controlled
with weaponless or baton tactics is needless use of force. Use
of a high-risk-of-injury tactic, if a practical alternative exists,
is needless use of force.

WHAT IS POLICE DEFENSE & CONTROL?

Police defense is not street fighting, combat or contest. The
techniques, training and practice, and, most important, the
attitudes suitable for police work are not those which are appropriate for street fighting, tournament sports or warfare.

In their search for a course of study which constitutes a solid,
socially acceptable, professional, effective method of weapon-

less defense and control, many police departments have gone through various phases of specialty training. Attempts have been made to turn police officers into boxing experts; attempts have been made to teach wrestling for police defense; attempts are now being made to apply karate methods, judo methods, aikido methods and combat tactics to police work.

As each specialty proves impractical, another expert is invited to demonstrate a specialty for police defense tactics. Because of expertise, each new demonstration of technique is dazzling to the audience. Whether the expert is demonstrating wrestling, boxing, judo, karate, aikido or jujitsu, the expert shows that the specialty "works." That specialty is then incorporated into the training program. And three years later the department or academy is again interviewing an expert who has the solution for the unsolved problem of what to teach police officers for defense and control.

The fallacy of the specialty approach to police work is that *all* specialties have drawbacks and weaknesses. No *one* specialty is effective for law enforcement unless the person using the specialty is an *expert. For the expert, it does not matter in the least which specialty is used.* Most police officers do not have the time, the training or the ability to become *experts.* Boxing for personal defense, which works extremely well for the trained, fast, fit individual with style and skill, is not useful for an individual who has had eight hours of boxing practice. It doesn't make any sense to claim for the specialty of boxing the same degree of efficiency when it is used by an expert as when it is used by an individual with a low level of skill. The same argument can be put forward with respect to the specialties of judo, wrestling, karate, aikido, etc. They are not effective unless a high degree of skill is achieved and maintained.

Complicated skills like judo and aikido are only effective when lightning-fast proficiency is achieved and it is possible to maintain such proficiency only through never-ending practice. The judo expert who stops practicing judo does not retain expertise; the aikido expert who does not practice does not remain an expert.

The alternative to the adoption of a *specialty* for police defense and control is the use of selected techniques from all the fighting skills. A small group of simple, effective defense tactics can be learned by *all* police officers, not merely by those of outstanding ability. A small group of effective, simple techniques can be remembered for operational use, whereas the complicated techniques are easily forgotten unless practice is continuous.

To be practical for police work, techniques must be easy to learn and remember, but it is a mistake to assume that what is simple and effective is also automatic. Self-defense tactics are not automatic actions; if they were, everyone would automatically respond to assault with an appropriate defense. Defense tactics, even the very easy techniques, must be learned and rehearsed.

A department considering a program of police defense and control should have a demonstration of the method as it can be performed by the average police recruit with the number of hours of training which *every* trainee will get. It is not practical to evaluate a defense method on the basis of what the specialist can demonstrate; he has practiced every day for years. His performance does not reflect the reality of police life. The performance of an expert is not relevant for the evaluation of a method to be used by police.

The reality of police life and work is that most officers get relatively few hours of instruction; they do not continue regular practice of the tactics and if they are lucky they will get a refresher course once or twice during their entire careers! Most officers apply defense tactics infrequently. They are not and cannot become experts. The defense method they learn must be practical at a functional level under the actual circumstances of police training and of police work.

WOMEN, JUVENILES, INSANE

Non-professional methods of coping with violence--retaliating in kind or using extreme countermeasures--are clearly seen to be inappropriate when they are used against women, youngsters and those individuals deemed incapable of reason.

However, the distinction between methods appropriate for "regular" police work and methods of dealing with the special cases disappears if the method itself is professional in orientation. Thus, if it is possible to deal with *any* individual using a range of tactics from verbal persuasion to mild coercion to moderate force to extreme physical force to use of baton to use of gun, then it follows logically that the same range of tactics can appropriately be used for the special cases.

It is only when needlessly violent tactics are used in the first place that it becomes necessary to invent a separate category of tactics for use with women, juveniles and insane persons.

CAN A NICE COP SURVIVE?

There is a tendency to confuse attitudes with procedures. A
friendly, nice-guy policeman who is not overly suspicious of the
people he comes in contact with is thought to be more vulnerable
to assault *because* he is a nice guy. Friendliness is confused with
carelessness.

An officer can be careful, prudent, alert, observant and self-
protecting without putting on a hostile or suspicious front. An
officer can be suspicious and yet be careless and vulnerable to
assault.

There are some situations in which no amount of precaution is
a guarantee of safety. There are a great many situations which
officers encounter every day in which routine procedures of preventive safety can minimize the danger of assault.

The choice is not between politeness and prudence; it is between
prudence and imprudence!

As knowledge accumulates about assault offenders and victims of
assault, it is impossible to avoid the conclusion that "victims" are
frequently accessories in the attacks upon them. While the layman
may be excused for feeling only sympathy for the victim and rage
at the offender, the police officer needs a different point of view
in order to deal with peace keeping duties. It is part of the
officer's job to remind the public that carelessness leads to vulnerability. When walking on well-lit, populated streets offers less
risk of assault than walking along dark, deserted streets, it is im-
prudent to walk along dark, deserted streets. When a woman
allows herself to be picked up by strange men and is then raped,
she may be thought to have contributed to the assault by putting herself in a vulnerable situation. When a man is mugged
and robbed in a dark alley, he may be thought to have contributed to the assault by putting himself in a vulnerable
situation.

Now if police officers accept the truth of the foregoing, and
most of you will, it is necessary to add that there are also instances of police assault in which the police officer contributed
to some degree--through carelessness, failing to follow proper
procedures or through poor evaluation of the situation.

DON'T DEPEND ON GUNS

Another factor which contributes to the vulnerability of police
officers is an unrealistic dependence on weapons.

Contrary to public misconception, derived mainly from TV and
the movies, officers rarely draw or use their guns in the daily
routine of work. The danger is that they accept the gun as having
protective properties, which, in many instances, it does not have.

Not only are you not permitted to draw your gun for many of the
situations you will encounter on the job but most of you would
not want to. Therefore, carrying the gun may result in an entirely
unrealistic sense of its worth and a dangerous sense of dependence
on it.

The best sharpshooter in the department may be the most
frustrated officer in those situations where the gun is useless.
Unless officers are equally adept at weaponless defense *and*
marksmanship they are not prepared with the fundamentals of
professional law enforcement.

THE POLICE PROFESSION: TO PROTECT AND TO SERVE

Doctors and police officers have many things in common. Both
are in service professions directed toward prevention and control
of distress. Both service professions require special training, but
both rely on human qualities which are functions of character
and personality.

Like the doctor, the police officer spends much of the working
day among people who are ill, in crisis, emotionally upset or
deranged. The doctor and the police officer spend much of their
time among people who are not presenting themselves at their
best.

The major part of a police officer's work does not involve that
entity which the general public thinks of as the "criminal" ele-
ment. Much of your work will involve people who are victims and
who need to be protected and helped. Many times you will find
yourself dealing with individuals whose unlawful behavior is
exceptional, not habitual; most of the time and in most situations
they are decent, law-abiding citizens.

The police officer, like the doctor, encounters frustrating situations for which there are no ideal solutions, sometimes not even

very good solutions, and sometimes even no solution. The suicide, the murder victim, the incurable--these are cases the doctor and police officer must deal with, often without hope of an agreeable solution.

There are other similarities. The day that a person earns the right to be called "Doctor" is only the beginning of the process which results in the development of a seasoned professional, though many years have been spent in preparation for that day. The day a recruit becomes an officer is the beginning of the seasoning process. Both professions depend heavily on experience for developing high competence in the practical applications of theoretical training and study.

This is not to imply that the training and education are wasted. On the contrary, as police work (and medicine) become more scientific and sophisticated, there is more and more for the recruit to learn before starting the postgraduate, in-service experience which results, finally, in a mature, experienced professional.

Professionalism begins with education and training. Professionalism is maintained through professional *attitudes.* Imagine a doctor who hates sick people, can't stand the sight of blood and inflicts unnecessary pain. Your judgment would be that such behavior and attitudes are wildly unprofessional and that such a person should not be a doctor.

You have chosen a profession in which there is considerable possibility that your clients will behave badly, foolishly or brutally. As a professional you will have to deal with these people calmly, intelligently and humanely. The worse your clients behave, the greater need there is for you to retain your objectivity and self-control. There is no rule which requires a doctor to *like* the patient, but feelings of dislike must not affect the quality of medical care. There is no rule that says you have to feel affection for people who are behaving badly, but that should not affect the quality of law enforcement you apply to them. The police officer who inflicts greater pain or suffering than is necessary is in the wrong line of work. The police officer who becomes another disputant in a dispute is not offering professional skill.

A professional method of doing police work will eventually earn the respect it deserves. In an ascending spiral, professional work is better for the community and it generates better attitudes toward the police. Professional methods of dispensing service are more efficient, safer and more rewarding.

PRE-INSTRUCTION

The material in this section is general preparation for the course.

OBJECTIVES: To define concepts of teaching and learning police defense and control tactics. To explain procedures and techniques of safe practice. To define the level of skill which is the course goal. To define the attitudes and procedures necessary for safe and efficient professional police work.

HOW TO USE THE TEXT

This manual has been prepared for use in academies, for recruit training and refresher courses, for college police science courses and for in-service programs.

The instructor who is familiar with practical police work and who is experienced in teaching physical skills will be able to adapt the material in the text to suit his style of teaching and to conform with departmental rules and regulations.

Of the many law enforcement agencies in the United States, a great number do not have access to formal instruction by experienced teachers of defense tactics for police work. Many of you do not have a choice between programs conducted by an experienced teacher or an untrained teacher; the choice is between having *no* program of defense tactics or of developing teachers out of your ranks. Many individual police officers will be using this book for independent study. It is to the developing teacher and to the individual that the following comments and information are directed.

WHO ARE THE TEACHERS?

A background of traditional karate, aikido, boxing, wrestling or judo is NOT a prerequisite for teaching defense tactics. Familiarity with police work and the ability to teach a physical skill (of any kind) are more important factors.

It is a mistake to assume that a person who holds a black belt in judo, karate or aikido is automatically qualified to teach police defense tactics. Black belts are awarded for excellence in performance, not for excellence in teaching. Tournament skills and teaching skills are not the same. Teaching requires the ability to communicate concepts, it requires patience, it requires tact and it requires the ability to help the students. None of these abilities is developed in contest.

Physical education teachers are usually more successful instructors than contest champions. If your department needs help in developing instructors of defense tactics, try to get it from individuals who know how to teach physical activities. A police officer and a physical education teacher, working together, can be a successful team.

OVERVIEW

First, read the entire book. Read the introductory material carefully. Skim through *all* the instruction; glance at all the photos. You should be acquainted with the attitudes, concepts and techniques in this course before physical practice begins.

In those departments where each officer can be issued a copy of the text, it can be used during training and retained for reference.

In those departments where the students will not be issued personal copies of the text, class sets, which are owned by the department, will be invaluable for the training program. When the student can read the material and study the photos of the techniques, it will facilitate and accelerate the learning process. Particularly if time is very limited, the instructor need not spend time in lecture but can assign reading to be done outside of class.

PRACTICE AREA & CLOTHES

The best practice area is a room without rugs, padding or mats. You do not need uniforms or special equipment. You will not be throwing each other onto the ground, you will not be practicing falling techniques and you will not do heavy calisthenics as part of your defense training.

For beginning practice, any loose, comfortable clothing is suitable. A sweat shirt and pants which allow freedom of movement make ideal training clothes. Tennis shoes should be worn for safety.

At least two of the final sessions of the training program should be done in full work uniform with regulation shoes and wearing all the equipment normal for daily duty. (For these sessions, guns should be checked by both partners to make certain they are not loaded.) The defense tactics must be possible to perform under the circumstances which prevail when you are on the job. Anything which cannot be done under those conditions is not practical police defense.

SAFETY IN PRACTICE

DO NOT BEGIN PRACTICE of the techniques until there is a
clear understanding of the safety procedures. There is no need
for anyone to be hurt in the process of training. There is nothing
to be gained from enduring unnecessary pain in the process of
learning the material. Police officers will engage in more vigorous
practice than laymen would, but when safety procedures are
understood and followed strictly, the possibility of injury is
minimized.

TAPPING FOR SAFETY

From the start, even when engaged in slow motion practice,
partners should use the tapping signal for safety. When a technique has been applied correctly and when you feel *slight* pain,
tap yourself, your partner or the floor as the "stop" signal.
It is much better to use the tapping signal than a vocal signal.
In a room full of people, "ouch" or "let go" might not be heard.

Stop the action *immediately* upon feeling the tapping signal.
It is very poor training procedure to allow partners to ignore the
signal to stop. It does not help the instruction to see how much
pain you can endure before tapping for release. Tapping is the
basic safety procedure.

1-3. An arm lock is applied. You tap yourself, your partner, or
the floor. Release must be immediate.

4. A neck hold is applied. Tap his arm for immediate release.

1

2

HOW MUCH REALISM?

Practice of the defense and control techniques cannot be altogether realistic--nor does it need to be. You are not trying to
prove that the tactics are effective, you are simply rehearsing
them for future use. For instance, you will concede, without
demonstrating the fact, that a sharp kick into the shin with the
edge of your service shoe is going to cause considerable pain.
When you go through the motions of a defense which begins
with a kick into the shin, you are not going to kick your partner
with force. But you will proceed in the defense sequence
as though he had been hurt by your kick. This is the only
practical way of learning self-defense without wrecking each
other. So not only do you simulate the defense, but your
partner simulates the likely reaction to your action. For instance, you may be told to begin a wrist grip release by kicking
into the shin. As you simulate a kick into the shin, your partner
should relax his grip somewhat because that is the most likely
reaction to your action.

The instructions in the text will occasionally remind you to
simulate a technique, but much of it is written to describe
operational use. In practice, do not make contact hand blows
and kicks. It is not necessary and it can be very painful. Imitate
the *gesture* of a forceful kick or hand blow, but stop before
making contact.

Be especially careful to simulate choking; be prepared to release
instantly at the tapping signal.

3   4

SLOW MOTION

A guarantee of safety in practice is slow motion practice of all new material. It is more important to learn a technique correctly than it is to do it quickly. Trying to apply operational speed at the same time that you are learning the technique may result in sloppy work and it may result in training accidents.

HORSEPLAY

The single greatest danger of accidents in practice arises from fooling around in horseplay. Defense and control tactics do work, they do cause pain and in some instances they do and *are intended* to result in injury--BUT NOT ON YOUR PRACTICE PARTNER!

In the field you would not let your adversary know what you were going to do; when you horse around with your partner, he *does* know what to expect and he is as prepared as you are to counter and resist.

LEFT & RIGHT PRACTICE

Most of the instruction in this book is shown on one side only. Practice the defenses reversing the instruction so that you develop the ability to use either right or left hand, right or left foot. Practice to apply a technique whether you are at the right or left side of the subject. Avoid dependence on the use of your strong side.

Adapt the techniques to right and left sides with special attention to protection of your gun side. If, as you practice a technique, it is clear that you are presenting your gun side to the subject, it is not a good technique for you. When you choose those techniques which will be your personal repertoire of defense tactics, eliminate those which do not adequately guard your gun side.

WHICH TECHNIQUES ARE FOR YOU?

All of the techniques in this course "work" in the sense that they are effective when used operationally. Some of them may not "work" for you, but they may "work" very well for other officers. Style of body movement, build, personal preference, previous experience in a fighting skill--all of these factors could affect your use of any specific technique.

There are more techniques of defense and control in the text than are needed by any single police officer. The material in the section on basic defense and control will prepare you to cope with most of the routine situations most of you will ever encounter. The reason for offering more techniques than you need is that you then have some choice in selecting what is best for *you* as an individual.

CORRECTING MISTAKES

Perfection of technique is not an objective of this course. The goal is functional, operational skill. If perfection of technique were required, only the exceptional trainee would finish the course. Make corrections when the errors invalidate the tactic. Make corrections when the errors result in vulnerability of the officer. Do not waste time correcting subtle errors of technique. The fine points of technical perfection have no significant value for police work.

The "subject" partner will usually be more aware of an error than will the practicing partner. Partners should be encouraged to correct each other.

STEP-BY-STEP

The most effective procedure for learning defense tactics is this sequence: First, practice each technique in slow motion, step-by-step as shown in the photos. As noted in the material on safety, slow motion of new techniques is a guard against training accidents. Slow motion practice of a new technique allows you to become familiar with what makes it work. You learn to drive a car slowly and correctly before you drive on the freeway.

When you are familiar with the way you move through the steps of a technique, eliminate the hesitations between the steps. Then begin to practice for smooth, flowing movements. You do not need lightening-fast actions to use this method but you must retain the concept of ongoing, continuous motion. When you can go through all the steps of a particular defense without hesitation and with the comfortable feeling of knowing you are doing it properly, then you may increase the speed of application.

Great speed in applying any defense tactic (of any style) is achieved by relatively few individuals. High speed is maintained only through constant practice. It is unlikely that many of you will continue to practice defense tactics throughout your working life. The defenses you are learning are effective when applied with moderate speed, and with a positive attitude.

COMBINING THE ACTIONS

Versatile, effective defense for police work is not achieved by learning a great many techniques but by learning a small group of actions well. By combining those actions to suit your own style and to suit the occasion, you have the ability to cope with a wide range of possibilities.

From the beginning, develop the attitude that there are only general guidelines for the way that defense actions are combined. If you allow yourself alternatives and options, you will avoid the trap of formalizing the work. Avoid rigid patterns of "he-does-this-I-do-that." Avoid thinking of any defense action "by the numbers." Instead, as you learn each technique, think of the various situations in which that technique might be useful. The more you are creative in the process of learning defense, the more ready you will be to cope with the reality of unrehearsed situations.

BE OBSERVANT

The two major elements in preventive defense are the following of correct procedures and a high degree of alertness to danger signals.

In handling domestic altercations, police officers have been hurt or killed by failing to approach with caution (the major cause of deaths), failing to check for guns, allowing one of the disputants to leave the room, making their own guns easily available to one of the disputants, getting in between the disputants, taking sides with one of the disputants, etc. It is not possible to list every mistake which might be made, but most errors can be categorized as failure to follow correct, cautious procedures and lack of alertness.

Whatever the situation, be cautious, observant, alert. Be on guard, ready to react, ready to move, ready to defend.

SAVE HIS FACE

Nobody likes to lose face. Men, especially, are touchy about losing face in front of neighbors, family or friends. The individual who reacts to frustration by fighting thinks that he is saving face by proving that he is a manly man.

Because you will be dealing with men who do not know how to handle their problems in a productive or positive way, you will have to help them avoid the resort of violence, at least for the moment.

The individual who only knows how to save face through proving his fighting superiority may *have* to assault you if you provoke or humiliate him. To submit meekly means more than loss of respect from his peers or his family; it means loss of self-respect as well.

Whenever you can, make it possible for the individual to comply with your orders in a way which appears to give him freedom of choice. When you want to remove someone from a touchy situation, try to do it by suggesting that you want to talk to him in neutral territory--away from the angry wife, out of hearing of the angry neighbor, or out of sight of the complainant. Take charge and take action, but avoid challenges and threats.

SELF-CONTROL FOR CONTROL

The public may (perhaps) be excused for harboring archaic attitudes about crime control, but professionals in law enforcement cannot afford the luxury of ignorance. The public reaction of rage against the offender is an understandable reaction. But it is only an outlet for emotion; rage is not productive of solutions for crime control. Strong emotions of anger, contempt, fear or vengeance interfere with police work.

The lay citizen may be excused for emotional responses to pain, suffering and crisis; the professional is expected to be in control of emotions which interfere with good judgment and good work. In the interest of a standard of police work, and in the interest of your physical safety, you must control your emotions.

Most of the individuals you will need to control by physical means will be confused, frightened, enraged or drunk. In many cases they will be incapable of normal or rational reactions to your actions, giving you an advantage. You are safest in situations of danger when you remain objective and when you push your "normal" feelings into the background. When you learn to control your own feelings, you give the appearance of someone who can *take control*. The troubled, deranged, confused or angry individual is made more emotionally upset by a show of emotion, but can often be cooled down by a quiet, calm show of authority.

Because many of the tactics of police defense are adapted from ancient Asian techniques, it has been suggested that the Eastern concept of inner tranquility should be adopted by police officers. The rare, exceptional individual may achieve inner tranquility in spite of money problems, health problems, housing problems, problems with children and four weeks of watch three, but most of us cannot do so. In my view, disciplined self-control depends on a conscious development of the *professional* attitude which allows you to push your feelings aside while you are on the job. This is what is expected of doctors, rescue workers, nurses *and* police officers.

SPORT FIGHTING

Sport fighting of any style has a useful place in police training programs--so long as sport fighting is not confused with tactics of police defense.

It is good to include boxing or wrestling in the training period
to give the recruit experience in body-contact fighting with rules.
None of the rules of sport fighting apply to police work, but the
give-and-take of sport fighting provides a background which is
generally helpful. Control of a struggling, violent individual is
not a sport, but sport work is a general introduction to the
notion of applying a fighting tactic against resistance.

Not the least benefit of boxing and wrestling in police programs
is the experience of getting hit or taken down to the ground.
A recruit who has taken a few punches during the training program is going to be a lot less nervous about the possibility that
he might get hit in the course of his duties. For people entering
a profession in which the possibility of assault is fairly high,
learning to take a blow without excessive fear or excessive rage
is an asset.

Judo is another possible sport activity useful in police work,
though not to be confused with practical tactics. Judo can only
be incorporated into relatively long training programs, whereas
boxing and wrestling can be introduced in relatively short programs. Unless students have spent a considerable time learning
the safety falls of judo, there is a high risk of injury in judo
practice.

FITNESS

Because it has been stated earlier that fitness is not a prerequisite of using practical defense tactics, it should not be
inferred that fitness is not important. *Peak* fitness, which is
a condition for tournament or contest, or which is a function
of age, cannot be expected of every officer. Only the exceptional individual retains peak fitness. It is generally assumed
that the only alternative to being in peak condition is to be in
terrible shape. There is another alternative: Stay in <u>good</u>
physical condition.

The recognition of fitness as a condition for police work
varies, but many departments do require a periodic health
examination. It would help considerably if more departments
would sponsor and encourage general activity programs. In
addition to encouraging and sponsoring an outstanding individual
to compete for sports honors, departments could organize
physical activity programs which would encourage general par-
ticipation.

Team sports, bicycle races, hiking groups sponsored by the department, and activity rooms with gym equipment reinforce the idea that physical fitness is valued.

STUDENT EVALUATION

Most students of defense and control will not, nor need not, achieve a high level of technical skill. An operational level of skill, a functional knowledge of the tactics is enough for most aspects of police work.

The operational skill of the students will depend chiefly on an understanding of the methods of defense and control and on attitudes. Understanding and attitudes can be roughly evaluated in the training program.

The trainee whose style of practice is lethargic, mechanical and without spirit may not be a good candidate for in-the-field police duty, though he may have excellent qualifications for other kinds of law enforcement work. The same might be said about the student whose style of practice indicates great reluctance to engage in body-contact activity.

The student whose practice of defense and control is careless or rough, who ignores the rules of safety or whose "retaliation" factor is high, may be demonstrating qualities which could translate into "brutality" in the field. If a trainee cannot control himself in practice with his fellow candidates or fellow officers, there is a high risk that he will have even less control on the street.

The student who practices with spirit and vigor, but who follows the rules of safety, is showing qualities which are valuable in the field. The student who can engage in vigorous practice with good self-control is showing qualities which are useful for police work.

WEAPONLESS DEFENSE & CONTROL

DEFENSE TACTICS: THE FUNDAMENTALS

The basic material of defense--hand and foot blows, parries, escapes, and combinations of tactics--is presented in this section.

OBJECTIVES: To distinguish between offensive and defensive use of tactics. To learn suitable hand and foot blows for defense. To distinguish between tactics which are appropriate for the layman on the street and those which have professional application for police duty. To learn the appropriate body targets used for hand and foot blows and to distinguish between minimum-risk and maximum-risk-of-injury body targets. To explain why some body target areas are suitable for police defense and why others should be avoided. To learn methods of deflecting, parrying and avoiding assault. To learn appropriate takedowns. To demonstrate examples of the applications of basic techniques and combinations of techniques.

OFFENSE/DEFENSE

It is not possible to define or distinguish between an offensive action and a defensive action by describing the technique used. The only way to distinguish between offensive and defensive actions is to know the circumstances. A hand blow may be used to begin an aggressive action, or it may be a way of deflecting or stopping an aggressive action. There is nothing inherently "offensive" or "defensive" in the hand blow. Exactly the same hand blow could be used defensively to stop an assault and then it could immediately become an offensive action if used to weaken or subdue the assailant. Exactly the same hand blow which began by being used defensively and then was used offensively might even shift into the category of "needless force" if it were used to hurt the subject to a greater degree than needed for control.

Hand and foot blows in police defense should be used defensively as much as possible. That is, their primary use is to deflect or stop an intended assault. The secondary use of those same hand and foot blows will involve weakening or hurting the assailant or subject as required to subdue and control. This is where the professional, ethical policeman stops.

It is not always necessary to use the three-stage sequence in defense and control. In instances where there is virtually no resistance, no hand or foot blows might be necessary; a control hold could be applied as the only needed action. In some cases, a hand or foot blow to stop the assault could be immediately followed by the control or restraint; no additional hand or foot blows would be needed for subduement. And in other cases, where resistance or assault is more serious, vigorous hand and foot blows to stop the assault would have to be followed by forceful hand and foot blows before a control hold or restraint could be applied.

HAND BLOWS

Open-hand blows are efficient. They are easy to learn and easy to remember; they allow flexibility of action. Hitting with the hand open requires less power than hitting with the fist. You can use open-hand blows against most basic target areas and hit effectively with less dependence on perfect accuracy. You need learn only a few methods of hitting with your open hand and you need learn only a few vulnerable body area targets to acquire functional, operational skill for your work.

One way of minimizing the possibility of having to use physical control is to avoid threats and challenges. Making a fist is a threat and a challenge. You can be prepared to use open-hand blows, if necessary, without the appearance of hostility. Once you make a fist, you admit that you cannot control the situation except with physical force.

The other disadvantage of using standard punching hand blows is that you must come within hitting distance in order to hit.

5. The partners shown here are roughly the same size and have about equal reach. To punch, they have to get within punching distance.

5

6. Using an open-hand blow, the partner shown left can stop the intended fist blow without putting his face within reach of his "adversary" partner's fist.

6

EDGE-OF-HAND BLOW (CHOP)

The outside edge of your hand is used to deliver the most effective open-hand blow. You strike with the fleshy area of the edge of the palm. You avoid hitting with any bony surface. When you hit correctly you do not strike with the finger or wrist bones.

To find the correct hitting position for your hand, strike lightly onto a table top or any other hard surface. Your hand is slightly cupped and tilted slightly downward, fingers are together, your thumb rests against your forefinger. Keep your hand firm but not rigid. If you strike correctly you will feel no bone impact. Adjust your hand position until you can hit the hard surface without feeling pain. When you achieve the correct position, you should be able to strike the surface with a full-power blow and feel only a tingling sensation.

The action of the blow is choppy and whipping; it is not a pounding action. In practice with your partner, do not make contact but simulate a vigorous, chopping blow toward the target area.

7. Strike back-handed, as though into the side of the neck.

8. Strike palm up, as though into the other side of the neck.

Practice left and right hand blows.

This hand blow will be used frequently throughout the text. It will be used for hitting and for blocking, for front and rear attacks.

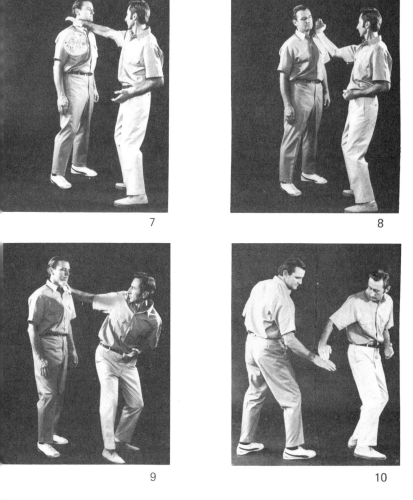

7

8

9

10

9. Practice using the open-hand blow to the rear. Without taking a step, turn your head as though responding to a cue, look at what you are hitting and strike as though into the face or side of the neck.

10. Practice the open-hand blow as though responding to a reaching hand, down and back.

Practice hitting to the right and left sides.

Look at your target as you hit. Move your head and upper body only.

11

HEEL-OF-PALM BLOW

11. There is limited use for this
blow, but it is extremely effective
where it is appropriate. Used with
vigor, this blow can hurt, disorient and put the assailant off
balance. It can be used with moderate force to push him back. It
can be used effectively by a smaller
officer against a considerably
larger individual. A vigorous blow
is delivered with thrust and with
arm follow-through. Strike up
under the chin.

ELBOW BLOWS

Use of the elbow for hitting is limited but extremely effective
when appropriate. You must be very close in to use the elbow.
The most likely application would be at an assailant to the rear.

12. Practice hitting with a raking action into the side of the head
or face.

13. With your partner standing behind you, turn your head and
without moving your feet, simulate a thrusting blow into his
midsection with your elbow. Hold your hand fisted, palm up.
This blow can also be used to hit up under the jaw.

14. Make a circular motion to simulate a blow around into the
side of the face or neck.

FOREARM THRUST

15. A short, thrusting action powers the forearm blow which
is used to move someone, to open an area or to separate people.
This technique is useful when you choose not to use the baton
nor to strike with greater force. If there is little or no resistance,
a pushing action against the upper chest or side of the neck is
effective.

16. When there is resistance, more thrust would be needed and
you could strike into the side of the neck for best effect.

12

13

14

15

16

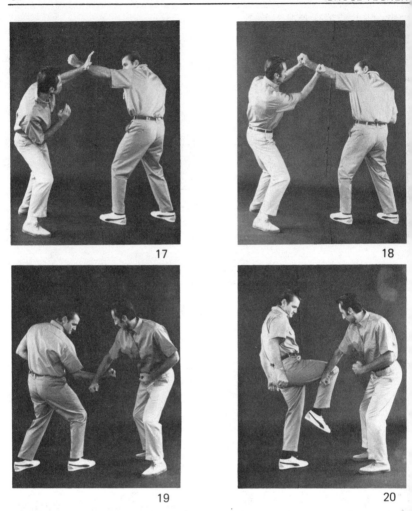

17 18 19 20

PARRIES: ONE-HANDED, TWO-HANDED, FOREARM

Parrying a forceful blow is safer and easier than blocking it.
You can use one-handed, two-handed, open or fisted-hand
parries or you can parry with the forearm.

17. Duck your head well out of range of the high punch as you
slash-parry a high fist blow. Practice parrying right and left blows.

Parry from the outside of the attacking arm or leg. Parries are
vigorous, thrusting actions with follow-through. In beginning
practice, your partner will telegraph his punches or kicks. When
you have practiced all the parries, your partner should speed up
his attack. To test your reaction, your partner can try to punch
you *on the shoulder.*

21

22

18. A two-handed parry is preferred by some. Practice one- and two-handed parries to find out which is more comfortable for you.

19. Parry low fist blows, using parry of your choice.

20. Practice parrying a knee kick with the forearm.

23

21. Parry the knee kick two-handed.

22. Parry the knee kick with a slapping, open-hand parry.

23. Parry a groin-level kick with the forearm.

24. Use two hands to parry the high kick.

24

25   26

BLOCKÍNG FOUR BLOWS: A TRAINING PROCEDURE

This is a procedure for learning to react to a punching blow with
a blocking response. It is highly unlikely that you would ever
block more than one or two blows.

25. Start slowly. Right partner simulates a high right blow which
you block with a slashing outward edge-of-hand blow.

26. He follows with a left punch which you block outward with
your right hand.

27. He simulates a right uppercut; you block down and outward.

28. You block his low, left punch with a right-handed slash
down and outward.

Do this, counting 1, 2, 3, 4 until you get the feel of the blocking
actions. Speed up the practice as you develop proficiency. With
moderate practice, you should be able to block four fairly fast
blows.

When you can stop the four consecutive blows in prearranged
order, your partner will mix his blows, trying to surprise you.

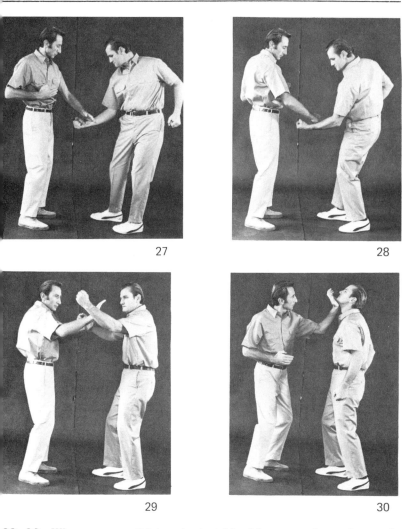

27

28

29

30

29, 30. When you are fairly adept at blocking several unrehearsed consecutive blows, practice blocking a single, unrehearsed blow followed by an immediate counter. In the example shown, a left-hand punch is blocked; the counter is a heel-of-palm hit under the jaw.

31

32

33

STEP AND DODGE

This is a practice procedure to counteract the common tendency to step forward *into* the adversary's hitting range. You are safer out of range of his fists and yet you can stop his attack.

31. For training purposes, your partner signals the attack by putting up his fists.

32. Step to the outside of the punching fist as you duck your head away.

33. Immediately follow this action with a hand or foot blow.

STOPPING A FIST ATTACK

As a practice procedure, invent and practice different combinations of material which you have covered thus far. Use *only* those tactics you have learned to this point.

Because many assaults are of the punching type, practice sequences of stopping a moderately serious and then a more serious fist attack. Parry the punching arm with a vigorous chop and then immediately follow this action with one hand blow for subduing. Parry the punching arm with a vigorous forearm blow and follow with one hand blow. Repeat the above combinations, but imagine that the resistance is greater and that your parry would have to be followed by two counter blows. Practice parry and dodge, step and parry, followed by several hand blows for weakening. Practice two-handed as well as one-handed parries.

The ability to stop a fist attack and subdue the assailant will give you the needed confidence to cope with this common type of assault. As you progress into the course, you will learn additional tactics to use in combination with the foregoing material and you will learn the necessary techniques of control and restraint which complete the sequence of defense/subdue/control.

IS KICKING BRUTAL?

Of the techniques which are presented in this text, the one most difficult to justify as "socially acceptable" is kicking for self-defense. Kicking has a bad reputation in the United States. In a street fight, if a man delivers a powerful punch to the head of his adversary, he is fighting "clean," but if he kicks him in the leg, he is fighting "dirty." The reactions are emotional and have little to do with the possible effect on the person being hit.

A forceful fist blow to the head can possibly result in serious or permanent brain injury. A forceful kick into the leg or knee could cause damage, too, but there is less risk of serious or permanent injury. Kicking can be the least forceful possible way of dealing with a violent individual. If kicking is used when it *is* the least forceful effective tactic, it is ethical. Police officers have a responsibility to justify forceful measures taken in defense and control. Just as you would have to explain the use of a weapon, you may have to explain the tactic of kicking. As part of the leadership taken by a professional police department, it may be necessary to help educate the community to a realistic view of ethical, justifiable tactics which can, in the long run, diminish the amount of force used in law enforcement.

34   35

36

EDGE-OF-SHOE SNAP KICK

This is the most efficient close-in kick. Draw your knee up and
cross-body to protect your groin; this positions your kicking foot
correctly. Deliver a snappy kick, using the edge of your shoe for
striking. Put the kicking foot back onto the ground as fast as
possible to avoid losing your balance. Aim at the knee or shin.

34. Draw your knee up, cross-body.

35. Snap outward with the edge of your shoe.

36. Practice the snap kick to the rear, aiming for the shin. In
your practice sessions, always turn to look where you are kicking.

LONG RANGE KICK

Against a dangerous individual you are most safe if you stay out
of his reach. Your goal is to stop him, hurt him as much as
possible without inflicting unnecessary injury and put him into
a vulnerable position for full control. The long range kick can
be the answer to the problem.

37. Pointing your supporting foot away from your partner, bend
and raise your kicking leg high, as shown.

38. Kick out toward your partner's knee, striking with the
bottom of your foot. The action is stamping, smashing. Recover
to the standing position immediately. The photo shows contact at
the knee, which can sprain or dislocate. The kick can also be
delivered into the side or back of the knee to buckle him down,
or you can kick into the shin.

39, 40. Practice the kick as a quick response to threat of attack from the rear. The purpose of this is to allow you to stop the attack without having to take a step around. At the cue of "attack" raise your kicking leg, turn your head to see your target and deliver a stamping kick back into the knee or shin.

Recover balance immediately. Check foot position; it should be horizontal to the ground on impact.

Avoid stepping in close to deliver the kick; you will lose the advantage of distance. Do not kick with the point of your toe; strike with the bottom of your shoe. Practice right and left side kicks. Your foot is horizontal to the ground on impact.

SCRAPE/STAMP

Using the edge of your shoe, scrape down the length of the shin and complete the action by stamping onto the top of the instep.

Avoid losing your balance by shifting your weight to the other leg as you begin the kick.

41. Begin the scraping action just below the knee.

42. Stamp onto the top of the foot. Recover.

43. Practice the same technique to the rear.

KICK BLOCKING

The most efficient defenses against high kicks are deflecting actions or moving out of the range of the kick. A forearm parry is effective against a high kick, but it is not a good idea to attempt to block or parry a low kick with your hands or arms. In order to parry a low kick you would have to place yourself in a vulnerable position with your head low.

44. A kick into the shin is an efficient tactic for stopping a toe kick. In practice with your partner, simulate this defense; the essential response of getting into position to kick at the attacking leg is more important than making contact. If you raise your foot into position for kicking, your partner will pull his kick and your objective is accomplished.

39

40

41

42

43

44

45   46

DISTRACTION & FEINTING

A tactic for diverting the attention of the adversary is a feinting blow. His reaction to your feint leaves him open for your next action. If you intend to use a hand blow as your major defense, distract him with a kick. If you intend to use a kick for your major technique, divert him with a high hand blow.

45. Deliver a high fist blow as a feint.

46. As he reacts to the fist blow, deliver a kick into the shin.

Subtle types of distraction--whispering, talking, finger wiggling, eye shifting--are used for diversion with weapon defenses.

Yelling or screaming is an excellent distraction tactic *where it is appropriate.* For the layman defending himself on the street, yelling is almost always appropriate; for the policeman it is not. There are times when you would not want to attract attention by yelling or when it would aggravate the situation to make noise. Don't underestimate the value of making noise when you can. Yipping as you go into action has the same effect as war whooping and baseball chattering--it disconcerts and disorients the assailant.

47   48

47. Deliver a feinting kick to the shin.

48. As he reacts to this, deliver your hand blow.

Depending on the circumstances, there are other methods of
effective distraction.

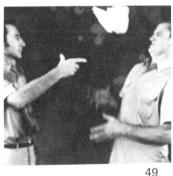

49

49. Throwing any object into the face is a good tactic. Even
when the object itself is not capable of hurting him, there is an
automatic drawing back from it. Even a handkerchief can be
used for this purpose. You may have other objects at hand, such
as pen, hat, coat, etc., or you may be able to pick up something
which can be thrown for distraction.

WHERE TO STRIKE: NERVE CENTERS & PRESSURE POINTS
FOR HAND & FOOT BLOWS

As they are used in this book, *nerve center* and *pressure point*
are terms of convenience; they are not anatomical entities.

Nerve center is used to describe body areas which are sensitive to
pain on most people because of a concentration of relatively
unprotected nerves. In this sense the shin is a nerve center.

Not all nerve centers carry impulses which are experienced as
pain. The buttocks have a high concentration of nerves, but as
it is ordinarily one of the least sensitive parts of the body, it
is not a nerve center for our purposes.

Pressure point is used here in a different sense from its use in
first aid. It will describe body areas which are peculiarly
vulnerable to injury. The windpipe is an example.

There is no way of categorizing a technique as "humane" or
"brutal" unless you consider the *effect* of the technique. The
same can be said of body target areas; you must know the
probable effect of striking at a particular spot in order to define
a blow to the area as "dangerous," "vicious," "moderate" or
"effective."

It is obvious, for instance, that stabbing finger blows into
the eyes are dangerous in the sense that very little force is required to effect serious, permanent eye injury. If you can control
a violent individual without using a "dangerous" technique, you
have the duty to do so.

Not all of the results of blows can be classified as easily as the
example just given. The effects of many blows can only be
described by taking into account relative size, fitness, emotional
condition and technical skill. In an operational situation you may
not have access to all the facts you would need in order to arrive
at a judgement. Therefore, you need to know which areas are
"good" body targets in the sense that they are effective with least
possibility of injury and which areas are "poor" body targets in
the sense that there is a high risk of injury.

Most of the instances in which you may have to use hand and foot
blows will require only one or two blows and those are only used
to allow you to apply a control hold.

Poor or inadequate training of police officers results in the ludicrous spectacle of officers exchanging blows with or struggling with a subject as though they were engaged in a street fight. Your purpose in using blows is not to win a fight, but to stop the assailant from hurting or assaulting you, and then to put him at a disadvantage in some way which allows you to effect control and transport. When a subject is extremely violent, it may not be possible to avoid injury but the possibility of serious injury or permanent disability should be minimized.

Preferred target areas are those which are most likely to be exposed and available. Preferred target areas are those which can be used by officers with functional rather than expert defense skills.

Against an actively assaulting or struggling subject, you may not have access to first-choice target areas and you must be prepared to strike at targets of opportunity--those areas which are exposed, not heavily protected by clothing and which are suitable targets in the particular circumstance.

PAIN VS. CONTROL

You must not rely on pain as the single factor for control. The techniques which rely on pain may be ineffective against a much larger, stronger individual in excellent physical condition. The techniques which rely on pain are ineffective against individuals who are in a state of rage or other emotional upset. The techniques which rely on pain may have to be applied with great force.

There are controlling techniques which cause pain but their effectiveness is due to other factors, such as putting the individual into weak balance, disorienting or confusing him, putting him on the ground or numbing him temporarily.

Officers encounter situations in which the assailant or subject is bigger or stronger, where the subject is smaller or weaker, or where the assailant is in an emotional or drugged condition. You must be prepared for all of these situations.

FRONT BODY TARGETS: PHOTO 50

a. EYES: Because the slightest contact blow or fingernail scratch to the eye might result in serious, permanent injury, disability or blindness, striking into the eyes is justified only when no other defense tactic would be effective or possible. Close in, against an extremely violent or vicious assailant, an unarmed officer might have to rely on finger stabs into the eye.

b. NOSE: An open hand blow down onto the nose results in pain and disorientation. Do not step in close to hit if you can avoid it, but if you are already in close, the nose is a good target area. The usual reaction to being hit on the nose is drawing the head back; eyes water, there is momentary confusion. His momentary confusion could allow you to apply a control hold. A forceful blow onto the nose might cause bleeding. Blood is bad press.

Hitting or pressing up under the nose is effective as a close-in technique. A smaller person can hit or press up under the nose of a considerably larger person. A sharp, vigorous heel-of-palm blow up under the nose can startle and disorient and place the individual in poor balance, or might even put him on the ground. A sufficiently forceful blow might draw blood.

Hitting up under the nose does *not* drive the nasal bones into the brain; that piece of misinformation derives from ignorance of human anatomy. The nasal bones are more fragile than the skull and there is no point at which the nasal bones could be driven into the brain area.

c. UNDER THE CHIN: A vigorous heel-of-palm blow up under the chin is effective for startling, disorienting and putting the person off balance. A forceful, unexpected blow could put him on the ground.

d. EAR: Behind the ears, in the hollows, is an area usually sensitive to pain. Placing the thumbs, fingers or knuckles into the hollows, you can cause pain by pressing or grinding upward.

e. JAW: An alternative to pressing up under the ears is the use of finger pressure up under the jaw.

f. SIDE OF THE NECK: At the side of the neck, between the ear lobe and shoulder, is a prime target area for defense and control. It is possible to effect pain, stunning or even unconsciousness with minimum danger of injury. (An unconscious person must have prompt medical attention.) A vigorous edge-of-hand blow into the side of the neck is one of the most effective techniques for defense.

AVOID THE HEAD. Any sufficiently forceful blow directed to the head can result in serious injury or could be fatal. It is not the specific target area which is hit, but the amount of force used which determines the seriousness of a blow into the head. Forceful blows to the head cause hemorrhage of brain blood vessels not because of the target hit, but because of the amount of power used. The temple area is commonly taught as a vulnerable area, when in fact the skull is thicker at the temple area than at surrounding parts of the head. It is only the degree of power used which determines the seriousness of a blow to the head.

There is another reason why police should avoid hitting at the head--blows to the head are either dangerous or ineffective. If you hit a man hard enough you can inflict serious injury; if you don't hit him hard enough, there is scarcely any result. This is especially true if the individual is enraged or drugged. You have all seen the photos of two or three policemen beating on someone (sometimes with batons) with no apparent effect.

Striking into the eyes is to be avoided except where a vicious close-in assault makes it appropriate. It might, in such situations, be more humane to use eye stabs than to use a gun.

Hitting onto the ears should be avoided. Moderate blows are not effective and powerful blows can cause injury.

AVOID THE WINDPIPE. Hitting or choking against the windpipe (Adam's apple) involves high risk of fatality.

Unlike the blow or hold applied against the side of the neck, the blow or choke against the front of the neck is difficult to apply with *controlled force.* If you render a person unconscious by applying pressure against the side of the neck, you need only be concerned about reviving him without delay as soon as he is under control. The individual who is rendered unconscious by a blow or hold applied against the front of the throat might be beyond reviving.

There are recent instances of individuals killed by windpipe chokes after having been stopped for minor infractions of the law. This is poor police training, reprehensible in terms of a life lost, and it serves to harden the stereotype of the police officer as a brute. There are enough effective, alternative control techniques available without having to resort to those with high lethal risk in situations involving minor infractions.

g. BEND OF ELBOW: Striking into the bend of the elbow hurts and bends the arm, deflects any blow and makes a control hold easier to apply. An edge-of-hand chop is effective.

h. FOREARM: At the mound of the forearm, about two inches below the elbow, is a concentration of nerves. Striking at this area results in pain, numbing and possible temporary paralysis. The effect of being struck with force at the mound of the forearm is similar to the effect of striking the crazy bone; there is a tingling pain and loss of strength in the arm. Depending on the size and condition of the person being struck and the size of the person hitting, the numbness may last for a few seconds up to many minutes. Having effected this temporary incapacity, it is easier to apply a control hold. Strike with the edge of the hand, using a sharp, snappy action.

i. BACK OF HAND: The back of the hand is usually sensitive to a grinding or pressing knuckle action.

j. UNDER LAST RIB: This area is sensitive in a special way. Most people are ticklish here, but it is easy to cause pain by digging or grinding into the fleshy area just below the last rib, using the knuckle.

k. KNEE: The knee is an ideal target for foot blows. It is vulnerable and it can be hit without getting into fist range of the assailant. Pain and temporary disability can be effected against a larger individual.

A kick into the knee (at a 45 degree angle is best) causes pain and could put the assailant off balance or onto the ground. A forceful kick can dislocate, disabling him. A sufficiently forceful kick could fracture.

l. SHIN: On most people, the shin bone is peculiarly vulnerable to pain. Without getting into fist range, the shin can be struck with a snap kick using the edge of the shoe, or with a stamp kick with the bottom of the shoe.

m. INSTEP: Stamping down onto the arched upper area of the foot causes considerable pain and can temporarily disable an assailant.

GROIN: Although hitting or kicking into the groin is a classical technique of old-fashioned self-defense, I do not favor this as a target area. Although it is very easy to cause excruciating pain by hitting into the groin, there are disadvantages which must be considered. There is a special connotation of brutality associated with hitting into the groin. It is necessary to come in very close to hit into the groin; it is safer to stop an intended assault from out of fist range if you can. Street fighters develop an automatic reaction to protect the groin. There are effective defense techniques for dealing with serious assault which are safer and more appropriate for professional police work.

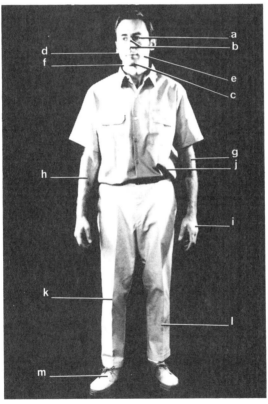

50

BACK BODY TARGETS: PHOTO 51

n. SIDE OF THE NECK

o. UPPER BACK: A vigorous *shove* against the upper back can cause loss of balance. The upper back is not a good target for striking blows. It is either dangerous or ineffective, depending on the relative size and strength of the individuals.

p. BACK OF KNEE: A vigorous kick into the back of the knee could put a violent assailant onto the ground. A slight, small person can kick into the knee of a larger assailant with enough force to be effective.

q. ACHILLES TENDON: The long tendon which extends from the calf to the heel is prominent and sensitive. An edge-of-shoe kick causes considerable pain.

In the movies the hero floors the villain using a chop to the base of the skull or onto the seventh vertebra. It "works" in films because the actors are paid to fall. Hitting at the base of the skull or the seventh vertebra is ineffective unless great force is used. It is altogether useless for a small person against a large individual. If a forceful blow is struck by a strong person against a small individual there is a high risk of serious, permanent injury.

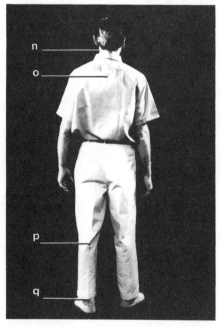

51

CONTACT & ACCURACY BLOWS: PRACTICE PROCEDURES

Contact hitting is difficult to practice without injury. To minimize the possibility of accidents, hitting and kicking must be simulated during the greater part of the course.

CONTACT BLOWS

52. Hand blows aimed into the partner's palm can be delivered with considerable force without danger of injury. This practice procedure is a way of hitting at a target using the various types of hand and arm blows.

Pad the end of a broomstick or long wooden pole using foam rubber or toweling fastened with tape. Do not fasten with pins or sharp metal of any kind. Partners take turns simulating "attack" with the pole.

53. Various hand blows can be practiced against the target. Practice right and left, high and low, hand and arm blows.

52   53

54   55

54. The padded pole can be moved around to simulate a moving target for the various kicking blows.

55. Kicks can also be practiced against a heavy punching bag, or you can improvise by filling a duffel or laundry bag with sand or wood shavings.

ACCURACY PRACTICE

Two pieces of easily improvised equipment can be used for accuracy practice. The first is the swinging ball. Make a hole through a three-inch rubber ball and insert a piece of rope or clothesline approximately six feet long. Make a knot.

If the training quarters allow, fasten the ball with pulleys so that it can be raised and lowered and will swing free. If you do not have such space available, students can take turns holding the ball at about shoulder height and then at about knee height.

56. Hit the ball *lightly* as many times in succession as possible. This is not power practice; it is for accuracy. If you hit too hard, the ball swings wildly. The goal is to increase the number of times you can hit the swinging ball using various hand blows and alternating right and left blows.

57. With the ball held at about knee height, practice to increase accuracy, kicking it lightly.

56

57

58

59

58. Secure a wire loop with tape at the end of a pole. Students take turns moving the pole about. Practice hand blows for accuracy.

59. Use the moving loop to practice kicking.

OFF BALANCE

Keeping yourself in strong balance is essential for effective
defense. Putting your subject off balance will assist you in
carrying out your defense.

Opposing force with force is not the efficient way of taking
an opponent off balance.

60. An individual who is pulling back is weak in that direction.
You can easily put him off balance by pushing him in the direction he is already going.

61. An individual pushing forward is easily put off balance by
pulling him further forward.

60

61

62. An individual running
away from you is most easily
put off balance by pushing
him sharply in the direction
in which he is moving.

62

ODY SPIN

f you are behind or at the side of a violent or struggling individ-
al, you are least vulnerable to assault and in the best position
o apply a control technique.

3. Right partner will be passive in beginning practice. You
tart facing. As you take the first step around to his side, hit his
eft shoulder with a vigorous palm or heel-of-palm thrust and
lap his right shoulder forward with your left hand.

4. Without hesitation, continue to step around behind him as
ou follow through with your arm action to turn him as much
s possible.

5. From this relatively safe position, you can apply control
old or takedown.

63

64

65

If the opponent is considerably bigger and stronger than you, the body spin may not turn him around, but it will put him in awkward balance and allow you to move around to his side or behind him.

66   67

66, 67. When the subject is a small person, the body spin might be the only defensive action you would need to use before taking a control hold.

KNEE-BUCKLE TAKEDOWN

Though you will not always need or want to put your subject on the ground, when dealing with vicious assault or violent resistance putting the assailant on the ground gives you a psychological advantage and it permits you to apply restraint more easily.

68. Partners start facing. Apply vigorous body spin action.

69. Follow through on the body spin. When you are in back of him, grab his right wrist with your right hand and grip his collar with your left hand. Kick into the back of his knee, pulling him back as you kick.

70. When he is completely off balance, a wheeling action of your arms will put him on the ground, face down. As he goes down, maintain your hold on his wrist.

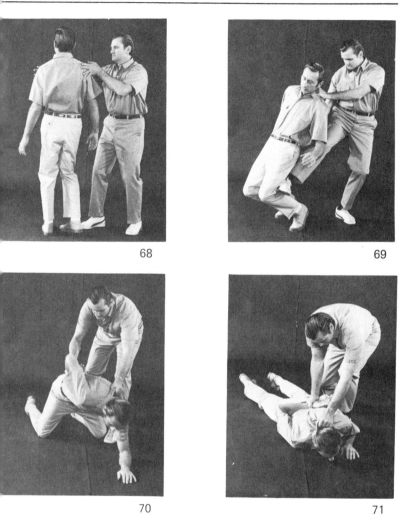

68

69

70

71

1. For complete control, ready to handcuff, pull the captured arm up his back as you move around to his head. Position yourself as far toward his head as you can--avoid standing where you could be kicked. From the position in photo 71 you can place your knee onto the back of his neck, freeing both of your hands to apply the handcuffs.

For operational use, you might have to precede the body spin with hand or foot blows.

STRAIGHT-LEG TRIP

The knee-buckle is the most simple and efficient takedown,
but if you cannot get behind the assailant, or if you cannot spin
him around, the straight-leg trip is a good takedown to apply
from the front. In practice, follow the step-by-step sequence
shown. In operational use, the takedown might be preceded
by hand or foot blows.

72. Grip his right arm with your left hand as you place the heel
of your palm up under his chin. Take a step forward with your
left foot.

73. Pivot on your left foot and shift body weight onto your
left leg. Extend your right leg so that it crosses behind his knee.

72

73

74

74. Pull sharply back with
your left hand as your right
hand pushes him back and
down, tripping him over your
extended leg.

Continue the twisting motion
so that he goes down and over
onto his face.

75   76

75. Grip his right wrist with your right hand.

76. Bend his captured arm up his back and push at his shoulder or head to keep him pinned while you step to place yourself at the side of his neck. Placing your knee on the back of his neck allows you to use both hands to handcuff.

STANCES: PRO AND CON

Most styles of sport fighting rely heavily on stances for tactical defense. For practical self-defense, stances have limited value. For law enforcement, stances have little positive value and can have a negative effect.

The ability to cool down a hostile individual is important for your safety. Taking an obvious on-guard stance is a signal that you expect physical violence. Taking an obvious fighting stance conveys the message that you are not able to cope with the situation except in physical terms. Negotiation, tact and verbal persuasion are no longer possible if you take a fighting stance or an obvious on-guard stance.

On the other hand, you do not want to place yourself in a vulnerable position in order to give the impression of being non-aggressive or hostile. If you put your hands in your pockets, behind your back, or on your hips, you are not fully prepared to defend yourself. Your hands should be out in front of you and your foot position should give you good, strong balance.

77   78

ALERT STANCES

The alert stances, which are non-obvious, non-hostile, on-guard
positions, give you the advantage of being prepared to defend
while you attempt to calm down and reason with the individual.

77. Your body is turned at a slight angle; your feet are shoulder-
width apart; your right (strong) side leads. Your left hand is
clasped over your right hand and pulls back; your right hand is
held open and pushes forward, creating a tension. There is
nothing about this stance to indicate that you are ready to fight.

78. If he moves to attack, you are ready to defend.

79   80

79. Your arms are folded and your hands are fisted, but the fists
are concealed by your arms. Your foot position gives you good
balance. Create a spring tension by pushing with your right
(strong side) arm. If he moves to attack, you are ready to hit
and kick, as in 78.

80. This position is one which many people unconsciously
assume when they are talking to someone. Use this in a *conscious*
manner as an alert stance. With your lead (strong) hand on your
chin and your other hand at your elbow, you give the impression
of calm neutrality. If he moves to attack, you are ready to hit
and kick, as in 78.

Any one of the foregoing is a good alert stance. Select the one
which feels most natural to you and make the conscious effort
to adopt it as a defensive habit.

81

STOPPING A FORWARD REACH

Many different kinds of aggressive actions begin with a reaching gesture. You do not need a separate defense against every specific assault which begins with reaching; you need know only one or two ways of stopping the action before it is completed. The techniques which follow are not intended to stop a violent assault or a punching attack; they are relatively mild ways of stopping an intended grab, push, pull, slap, claw or poke.

81. Your partner, shown right, clues the attack by reaching out. Slash down onto both his arms.

82, 83. Attacking partner, shown left, reaches out. Clasp your hands together (do not intertwine your fingers) and thrust sharply upward and follow through. Your hands and forearms form an inverted "V."

82

83

84

85

4, 85. A clawing, reaching action can be diverted with a slapping
arry against one arm.

ny of the foregoing might be enough to handle a mild situation.
)r, you might follow up with hand and foot blows, or you could
se a control hold after having stopped the intended assault.

ACK ATTACK: AWARENESS PROCEDURES

)evelop the habit of being alert to faint cues of possible danger
f back attack. Although you should be able to defend against
ack attacks, you are less vulnerable if you can react before the
ntended action is completed.

ecome aware of sight, sound and touch clues which indicate
 threat.

mong the visual clues are shadows, movement seen in peripheral
sion (out of the corner of your eye), changes of light values and
flections. Faint sounds might indicate the presence of someone
ehind you--slight shuffling, crackling, breathing, etc. React to
ne merest suggestion of touch, turning your head to see what is
appening.

86   **87**

86. Your partner stands behind you and gives you faint clues of "attack." He may touch you very lightly, or wiggle his fingers just within your peripheral vision, or he may move his foot forward with a faint shuffling. If a class is practicing, it is difficul to hear the sound clues and you may have to practice only the touch and sight responses.

87. At his cue, turn your head to see what is happening as you block in a defensive, guarding action. Do not step or move your feet. The purpose of this procedure is to practice the quickest possible response.

88. After you have practiced the look and block, practice the triple simultaneous actions of turning your head to look as you block and kick. Do not take a step with your non-kicking foot.

You are more protected if you *can* take a step away and face the threat, but the foregoing procedure is practice to react quickly when you might not be able to turn your body or take a step.

88

SCAPES & RELEASES

Most of the techniques in this course are based on the assumption
that you do not need to wait for an assault to be completed to
defend yourself. It is more efficient to stop the assault at the
attempt stage. Correct preventive procedures will minimize
the possibility of surprise attack, but you should know how to
cope with chokes, grips and pins if they are taken.

BACK GRAB RELEASE

9. Back grab has been effected,
over the arms. Kick into the shin
as you clasp your hands together
and take a deep breath, expand-
ing your chest fully.

89

90

91

0. Exhale sharply and duck down to loosen his grip. Hit into
the midsection with your elbow. When you are free, step away
and face him.

1. If the grab is under the arms, use an elbow blow into the
face and kick into the shin. Repeat as necessary to escape.

92   93

FOREARM CHOKE RELEASE

92. Back choke has been effected, bending you back as shown.

93. *Do not struggle forward* against the choke as this would only intensify the pain. Turn your head into the bend of his elbow and grip his arm at the wrist and elbow, jerking down on it sharply. This will not break the choke but will allow you some relief so that you can carry through with your defense. Kick vigorously into the shin.

94. Continue to kick forcefully into the shin as you maintain your hold on his arm.

95, 96. When you feel his grip is looser as the result of your kicks, step *back* and *under* his grip.

97, 98. As you step back, maintain your grip on his arm and complete the action by pulling his captured arm up his back.

94

95

96

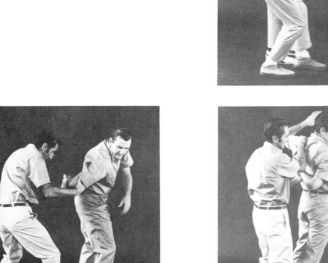

97

98

99

100

101

102

WRIST GRIP RELEASE

99. Both your wrists are gripped from the rear. Kick into the shin.

100. Snap one hand free, pulling it out from between the thumb and forefinger (the weakest part of his grip). This is an easier escape than trying to free both wrists at once.

101. Hit with the freed hand or elbow.

102. Turn. . .

03. and hit. Continue as
ecessary.

103

ARM PIN RELEASE

104. Both arms are pinned. (If there are two assailants and one
s holding you in a pin, your first action would be vigorous kicks
against the man whose hands are free to hit you.) To break the
rip of the man holding you, kick into the shin, and then. . .

05. turn your upper body sharply to the right. This will have
he effect of tightening his grip on your left arm and reducing
is grip on your right arm.

104

105

106

107

108

106, 107. Jerk your right arm upward (not forward) as you turn counterclockwise.

108. Continue hand and foot blows as necessary.

Practice the escape from the left side.

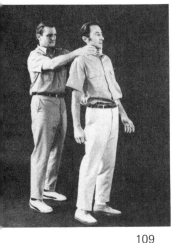

109

110

111

FINGER CHOKE RELEASE

109-111. Finger choke has been effected from the back. Grip his little fingers and break the choke with a snappy outward action, then step away and hit and kick as necessary.

The same technique of breaking a grip by pulling at the little fingers (or finger) can be used for many other situations. It is easier to exert effective pressure against one finger than it is to try to pry all the fingers loose. Experiment with your partner. Allow him to grip your shoulder in a firm grip. He cannot resist if you pull out and back on his little finger, though you might not be able to break his grip if you attempt to *pry* his hand away. Work carefully. A jerky action against the little finger can dislocate it.

112

113

FULL NELSON ESCAPE

112. Neck lock has been applied.

113. Clasp your hands together and push back against your own forehead to reduce the pressure of his grip. Kick with vigor into his shin. Repeat as needed to loosen his grip.

114. Scrape down his shin and stamp on the instep if necessary.

115. When he has been hurt by the kicks, step to the side and back with your right foot.

116. Place your left leg behind his right leg.

117. Buckle his right knee with your left knee as you deliver a back-handed arm or hand blow. The combination of knee buckle and hand blow should take him down.

114

115

116

117

118

119

DEFENSE FROM GROUND

If you have been put on the ground, avoid getting up within
kicking range. It is safer to defend from the ground than it is
to put your head within punching or kicking range.

118. If you are on the ground and the assailant is standing, keep
your head away from him. Pivot on your buttocks, using your
hands to move about. Your head should be raised. Kick with
one or both feet, following his movements. Kick vigorously,
low into the shins. Do not attempt to rise until you have hurt
or disabled him.

119. Move back as you come up onto your feet.

120. Avoid moving toward him as you rise.

120

121   122

121. If you have fallen or been knocked down and the assailant
s at your side or straddling your body, use hand blows.

You might need to use moderately forceful blows, such as
shown here . . .

122. or you might have to use stabbing finger blows into the
throat or eyes of a dangerous assailant.

STOPPING A FIGHT

123. Avoid, if possible, coming between the two individuals
fighting. You can control the situation more effectively by
approaching from the back and you are less likely to get hit.
Avoid the mistake of immobilizing one person; that only makes
it easier for the other man to hit him.

124. Use the body spin to wheel one man around and thrust
him out of range.

123   124

125. Immediately use the body spin on the second man.

Once they are separated, you have a better chance of taking control of the situation.

125

TWO ASSAILANTS

If you have time in which to evaluate which of two assailants is in charge, stop him first. If you cannot determine which man leads, stop the larger man first. If there is no opportunity to select the bigger man or the leader, stop the closer one.

126-129. Two assailants are directly facing you. Both are moving in, but the man on the right is taking the lead. Kick the leader and move around to his side as you apply a hand blow or a second kick. Keep moving to put him between you and the second man.

130-133. Push the first man into the second man, then kick the second man and move around behind him to apply a hand blow or a second kick. Push him into the first man.

126

127

128

129

130

131

132

133

134

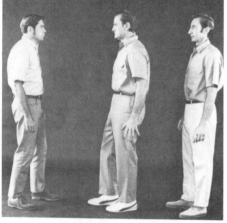

135

The essential elements of this defense are keeping in motion and staying out to the side or behind the assailants. Do not allow yourself to get in between them if you can avoid it.

134, 135. You get caught between two assailants, one at each side or one in front and one in back.

136. Begin your defense with simultaneous blows. Kick one man and hit the other.

137. Quickly reverse the actions to kick the man you have hit and hit the man you have kicked.

138. Move around behind the person who appears to offer the least threat.

139. Use him as a shield and push him into the other person.

140. Continue with kicks and hand blows as necessary to subdue.

136

137

138

139

140

CONTROL TACTICS

The control holds which are appropriate for police work form a
small group of tactics ranging from minimum to maximum control
and restraint. These few tactics can be used flexibly to deal with
most of the situations most of you will ever encounter in the
daily routine.

OBJECTIVES: To learn appropriate techniques of police holds
and come-alongs which can be applied to situations ranging
from minimum to maximum resistance. To learn restraint techniques which do not rely solely on pain. To distinguish between
high-risk-of-injury choke holds and holds for maximum control
with least risk of serious injury. To learn to apply holds in motion
and to learn to recover from error. To learn a flexible sequence
from guide-along to come-along to moderate restraint to full-
control holds.

GRIPS

141. NATURAL GRIP. When you are instructed to take a
natural grip, reach forward as though to shake hands and grip
with your thumb at the top of the grip.

142. UNNATURAL GRIP. Turn your hand so that you grip
with the thumb at the bottom of the grip.

BASIC ARM BAR

This control technique is simple and effective. It can be used in
a wide range of situations. It can be applied in a moderate way
when appropriate; a more vigorous application is possible when
necessary.

143. Step around to his right side and slash down onto his
fight forearm.

144, 145. Grip his right wrist with your right hand and turn his
arm so that his elbow is up; place the edge of your forearm onto
the back of his elbow.

146. Step back into strong balance. Apply pressure against his
elbow with your forearm as you pull back and up on his wrist.
If the individual is not offering much resistance, only moderate
pressure is needed for control. If he is more difficult to control,
you might need to hit down onto his elbow with your forearm to
effect submission.

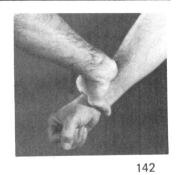

141

142

143

144

145

146

The basic arm bar can be applied from either side. With minimum practice you should develop enough skill to allow you to use it from the right or the left side with equal ease. While you are taking the hold you are around to the side of the person, rather than in front of him. When you have taken the hold, you are controlling him from the side and to his rear, giving you the greatest degree of protection.

When the hold is taken you can lever him down to the ground, you can walk him or you can maneuver him into position for putting on handcuffs.

The various ways in which the arm bar could be used will be described further along in the course. At this point you are learning the basic actions. Your partner is passive and allows you to practice without resistance or opposition. Right partner signals assault by reaching out.

Practice the basic actions from right side and left side until you can apply the arm bar with ease from either side.

You do not have to develop lightning-fast reactions to use this technique effectively. Learn to do it correctly and develop the habit of working smoothly and continuously. If you keep moving, moderate speed is enough.

On the job, when the hold is taken, you would immediately move into the next step--putting him on the ground, walking him or disarming him--as will be shown in the defense examples.

Make certain that you do not present your gun side to his free hand.

WRIST LOCK

The wrist lock has the advantage of being less visible than the arm bar or the rear bent-arm lock. It is particularly appropriate for control of subjects who are offering ineffectual resistance--a drunken person, a weak individual or a woman, for instance.

147. Grip his elbow with your left hand and place the palm of your right hand at the back of his hand.

148. Bend his captured hand double as you bend his arm so that his forearm is horizontal.

147

148

149

150

149. Slide your left arm under his captured arm, locking his elbow into your side and place your left hand at the back of your own right hand.

150. Apply pressure by clamping into your body with your elbow as you push his captured hand toward his elbow. Keep him moving as you apply the pressure.

When you have firm control, you can, if you need to, maintain the pressure with your left hand, freeing your right hand for other use.

151   152

REAR BENT-ARM LOCK

The rear bent-arm lock can be applied as the control hold of first
choice, or it can be used as a recovery from an attempted arm
bar. If you have made a mistake in the application of the arm
bar, or if the subject succeeds in pulling his arm into his side,
you can use his action to help you regain control.

You apply basic arm bar and allow your partner to pull his arm
toward his side.

151. Instead of struggling against his action, pull his captured
wrist back.

152. Pull his arm up behind him, pressing or hitting his bent arm
at the elbow to assist your action.

153. Place your left hand on his left shoulder for leverage.

154. Apply pressure by lifting his bent arm and pulling back
with your left hand. You can walk him forward from this position or take him to the ground.

153

154

BASIC GUIDE-ALONG

Police officers can develop some aspects of professional skill only through experience. There is no way to *teach* you when you should avoid touching a person who *might* have to be taken into custody (or removed from a situation) nor is there a simple rule to help you. The decision to put your hands on an individual or to avoid putting your hands on him will depend on a complex combination of factors which you will have to evaluate.

Your manner of approach and your general demeanor can have a great deal to do with how a specific situation develops. You can proceed in such a way as to inflame a touchy individual or you can handle him in a way which cools him down. There are many instances in which you can only evaluate the potential of a situation after you have talked with the person or people involved. Even when you do not anticipate physical assault, you will make your approach with caution, with the least show of hostility, with a demeanor of calm authority and with readiness to cope with any development.

155   156

155. Whenever possible, approach the individual at an angle
off to his right side. Most people are right-handed and you may
want to control his right arm. Keep a short distance away; be
close enough to grip his arm, if necessary, but not so close that
you appear threatening.

156. You make the decision to lead him away or you evaluate
the situation as one from which he may try to leave. He is not
being actively assaultive or belligerent, but he is not entirely
cooperative. Keeping your gun side away from him, grip his
elbow lightly. Continue talking. Anything you say to indicate
that you are in charge, but not hostile, will be helpful at this
point --"Come over here and tell me your side of it" or "Let's
go where we can talk about this," for instance.

157. The next degree of control which still shows little indication
of coercion is the guide-along. In the guide-along position, you
remain cautious and observant, ready to respond to serious
resistance or assault.

158. If he begins to offer some resistance to your guiding action,
you can apply moderate pressure at his elbow as you pull back
slightly at his captured wrist.

159. If necessary, you can easily apply the arm bar with as much
force as is needed for control.

160, 161. If he pulls his arm forward from the arm bar, you can
switch to the wrist control hold.

157

158

159

160

161

162

163

164

162-164. Or if he attempts to twist out from the arm bar, you can easily apply the rear arm lock.

CHOKE HOLD PRACTICE SAFETY

The choke hold and neck lock controls which follow must be practiced exactly as outlined in the instruction.

Two factors will insure safety in practice: immediate release at the tapping signal and correct placement of the forearm when applying pressure.

165

165. Pressure for the choke hold control is applied at the *side of the neck*--at the carotid artery.

166

AVOID THIS

166. Pressure applied at the front of the throat, at the windpipe, quickly subdues the individual, but at the risk of serious or fatal injury! Against a struggling individual, it is very difficult to limit the amount of pressure to just enough for submission. A forceful blow or pressure applied with a snappy action against the windpipe can cause rupture and death. In training practice, partners may injure each other if the windpipe strangle is applied instead of the carotid artery choke.

NECK LOCK CONTROL: AGAINST CAROTID ARTERY

Pressure applied against the carotid artery is efficient and humane. Unlike the choke against the windpipe, this technique is highly unlikely to result in permanent or serious injury. An individual struggling against pressure on his windpipe can be killed in the process of struggling; when an individual struggles against pressure at the carotid artery he may lose consciousness. Prolonged unconsciousness is dangerous, but the unconscious individual can easily be taken into custody and given medical care.

In application of the carotid choke hold there will be variation of effect depending on the amount and accuracy of pressure and depending on the subject's physique and state of health. Moderate pressure against the carotid artery usually makes the subject light-headed, confused and disoriented. The force required to render a subject unconscious would vary from person to person. This is a particularly effective tactic for controlling a violent individual who does not respond to pain.

167. Start by facing your partner. Step to his right side as you place your left hand just above his elbow.

168. Push his arm cross-body as you take another step around him and place your right forearm against the left side of his neck. Check your arm position here; your forearm must *not* be placed at the front of his throat. Grip cloth with your right hand.

169. Take another step around to place yourself behind him and grip his left wrist.

170. Apply pressure against the side of his neck (carotid artery) with your forearm, as you pull his captured arm back and across your chest.

From this position you can move him with the greatest degree of control by walking him backward or you could put him on the ground.

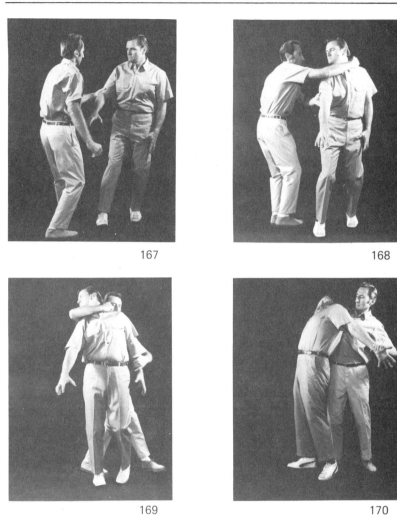

167

168

169

170

Against strong resistance you could strike a vigorous forearm blow into the side of the neck and then apply the control hold.

171

172

173

171-173. The principle of moving from a milder to a more
forceful tactic can be applied as in this example. A violently
insane person, for instance, might struggle out of a control hold
first applied and then you might use the carotid control hold
for submission.

Practice this control hold in very slow motion. Your partner will
offer no resistance and you will be especially careful in beginning
practice to avoid putting pressure against his windpipe. Use the
tapping signal at the first indication of pain; release pressure
immediately upon the tapping signal.

174

175

176

177

VARIATION OF NECK LOCK CONTROL

174. Partners start facing. Left partner signals assault by reaching high with his right hand. As he reaches, take a step forward as you deflect his reaching arm with a snappy heel-of-palm parry.

175. Take another step as you slide your right hand under his raised arm.

176. Continue stepping around in back of him as you place your right forearm at the side of his neck . . .

177. and grip your right fist with your left hand.

178

178. Apply pressure by levering into the side of his neck with your forearm. By grinding your forearm into the side of the neck you can apply additional pressure. Keep him moving. Keep him off balance by leaning forward slightly as you walk, staying behind him.

APPLYING HOLDS WALKING: A PRACTICE PROCEDURE

After you have learned the control holds from a standstill, practice them moving to approach a more realistic situation.

The procedure should be practiced from the right side and the left side. The walking application should be practiced using all the control holds you have learned.

179

180

181

179-181. Partners start a few steps away from each other. As the "suspect" partner walks forward, you walk toward him and time the application of the hold so that you can do it at the appropriate time. If you start too soon you will be in an awkward position; if he goes completely past you, of course it is too late.

Practice applying the holds on your partner when he is walking in front of you.

182   183

184   185

FRONT BENT-ARM LOCK

This hold is especially useful as a recovery from an unsuccessful attempt to apply an arm bar or wrist lock.

182. Apply a basic arm bar or wrist lock and then allow your partner to pull his arm away.

183. Without letting go of his wrist, push his arm into the bent position as you prepare to grip your own right wrist with your left hand.

184, 185. As you grip your wrist, pivot so that your body follows the arm action and you will be at his side with your right elbow ready to lever or hit, if necessary. From this position you can walk him backwards or you can put your right foot behind his right foot and take him down.

SEARCH & ARREST
PRISONER TRANSPORT
INSTITUTIONAL CONTROL

OBJECTIVES: To learn the prudent, safe procedures for searching a suspect. To learn handcuffing procedures including handcuffing against resistance and cuffing on the ground. To apply previously learned defense and control tactics to typical law enforcement duties: How to remove an individual from a vehicle and how to place resisting individuals into a vehicle for transport. How to control prisoners resisting passively. How to control prisoners offering moderate resistance. How to cope with assault and fighting in the cell. How to use a blanket for control of a violent individual.

SEARCH PROCEDURES

186. A secure search position is with the suspect's hands away from his body, either at the back of his head, as shown, or on the top of his head, or with his hands raised. His feet should be spread and he should be somewhat bowed back to put him in weak balance. In this position his hands are immobilized, he is unable to brace himself and you have good control.

187. For dealing with a suspect who might be more dangerous or if you have more than one individual to search, use the crossed-leg kneeling position.

186

187

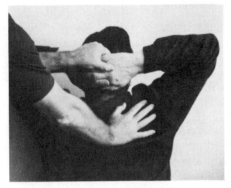

188

Position yourself at his side to be able to watch him front and back. Keep one hand at his upper back or shoulder . . .

188. or over his clasped hands as you search with the other.

189. The old standard police search posture with arms braced against a wall or car has the disadvantage of allowing the suspect to use one hand easily while he braces himself with the other. Instances of police officers shot while searching in this manner have drawn attention to the drawbacks of the old standard posture.

190. To search a standing suspect with his hands raised, keep one hand on his shoulder and be prepared to pull him off balance backwards, if necessary.

There is maximum protection against a highly dangerous suspect if the individual is prone (face down) on the ground. The officer has to use his judgment to determine when the prone search would be appropriate.

NOT RECOMMENDED   189   190

HANDCUFFS

Handcuffing procedures are subject to variations in department
regulations. Increasingly, modern concepts of law enforcement
include concern for the feelings of suspects and prisoners. Care
is taken to avoid needless public exposure of handcuffed individuals.

If front handcuffing is used, greater security can be insured by
cuffing with the backs of the hands together, rather than with
palms in. With palms out, there is less flexibility of arm movement.

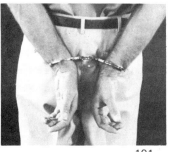

191   192

191. The most secure manner of cuffing is with the hands behind
the back, palms out. Place the cuffs so that the locks are up; it
is awkward to unlock cuffs when the locks are underneath.

192. A double-locked cuff is safer and gives greater security. A
double-locked cuff prevents injury to the wrist and is harder
to pick. Against a struggling individual it may be difficult to
double lock the cuffs, but once he is calmed down you can adjust
the cuffs to the proper diameter and double lock them.

193. For maximum security the cuffs can be applied with links
passed under the belt.

194. He can be handcuffed to a chair.

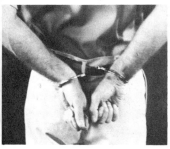

193   194

195   196

195. If you need to cuff two individuals and can apply two pairs of handcuffs, the method shown gives the maximum security.

196. When handcuffs are not available, temporary restraint can be applied by pulling the coat or jacket halfway down the arms. Twist and bind the jacket to secure it and propel him forward.

Plastic handcuff straps are being used in some departments, though they are not acceptable in others. The plastic cuffs can be used only once and then are destroyed in the removal. Plastic handcuffs can easily cut a struggling individual. They are not suitable for prolonged holding because they are easier to escape from than metal cuffs. The advantage of plastic cuff straps is that more than one set can easily be carried by the police officer. Plastic cuffs are faster to apply than metal cuffs and it is possible to link several individuals for temporary holding.

HANDCUFFING AGAINST RESISTANCE

197. To apply handcuffs against a resisting individual, slash down onto the forearm or into the elbow to weaken that arm.

198. Kick into the shin to distract him as you grip his weakened arm, pull it sharply forward and cuff that wrist. DO NOT hit the wrist with the cuff; place into position and press to secure.

199, 200. Yank down on his cuffed wrist as you step behind him and grip his left shoulder and pull back sharply.

201. Apply second cuff, using a kick into the back of the knee if necessary.

197

198

199

200

201

202   203

CUFFING ON THE GROUND

202. If you need to take a subject down, you will want to place him prone (face down) for easier control. Should he go down on his back, immediately cuff the near wrist and pull the cuffed arm toward you as you push his head away from you, wheeling him over onto his right side so that you can grasp his left arm.

203. Secure handcuffs.

REMOVAL FROM VEHICLE/CAROTID CONTROL HOLD

This technique is a variation of the choke control hold against the carotid artery. Pressure is applied at the side of the neck, but the leverage is applied in a somewhat different manner. The individual in this situation is resisting passively.

204. With your left hand grip cloth at the back of his collar (or in that general area) placing your forearm against the side of his neck. With your right hand, grip cloth at the back of his upper arm. Pressure is applied by a scissoring action. Your left hand pulls in and down; your right hand pushes up and across.

205. Close-up of the hold.

Apply pressure and remove the subject by pulling upward and out. As he is being pulled out, twist him so that his back is toward you, bracing him against the car. The hold can be maintained without coming into close body contact while you give verbal instructions, allowing you to search or handcuff.

Remember that you must keep moving. Continuous, uninterrupted, flowing actions are more important than speed.

REMOVAL FROM VEHICLE/ARM BAR & TWIST

206. The individual is resisting removal by holding onto the steering wheel. Reach in and strike into the back of this hand with an extended knuckle and quickly follow this action with a slash onto the forearm nerve or into the side of the neck. Repeat, if necessary, to weaken his grip. Close-up of hand blows, 207.

208. Grip his left wrist with your left hand (your thumb down) and pull his captured arm sharply toward you, twisting it clock-

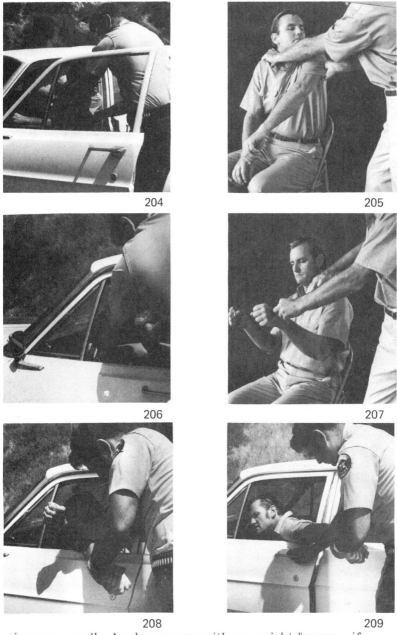

204

205

206

207

208

209

wise as you pull. Apply pressure with your right forearm, if
necessary, to allow you to continue the removal.

209. Maintaining the twisting/pulling pressure on his captured
arm, open the door with your right hand, bracing him into the
side of the door. Use the door as leverage to pull him further
out of the vehicle.

210

211

210. When he is partly removed, grip the back of his collar with your right hand and twist his captured arm upward.

211. If considerable resistance continues, kick behind his knee to buckle him.

To prepare to handcuff, lever him against the side of the car, pushing his captured arm up his back.

212

213

PLACING INTO VEHICLE/CAROTID CONTROL HOLD

212. Subject actively resists being placed into the vehicle. Slash his arms. Kick if necessary.

213. Apply the carotid choke control hold, making sure that you place yourself in the least vulnerable position--to the side and somewhat behind him.

214.

214. Using your whole body as a lever, wheel him around,
off balance and down. Maintain the pressure to get him into
the vehicle.

NOTE: The officer shown in this sequence is left-handed and is
correctly applying the hold to keep his revolver out of reach of
the subject. The safe application of this hold is with the subject
on the opposite side of your weapon.

ARM BAR

215. Subject actively resists placement in vehicle. You distract
and divert by a thrusting gesture toward his face as you kick into
the shin.

216. Use the body spin to thrust him against the car.

215

216

217

218

217. Brace him with one hand and kick into the back of his knee as you open the car door.

218. Use the basic arm bar or variation to apply pressure to put him into the vehicle.

HANDCUFFED

219. Once handcuffed an individual may become totally compliant or he may become frantic and struggle against being put in the vehicle. Do not struggle against the struggling subject; force is not the most effective way of subduing him. Rather, apply pressure by pulling upward on his captured wrists as you pull downward at his collar, shoulder or hair and lever him into the vehicle.

220. If necessary, kick into the knee to prevent him from kicking you.

219

220

TWO SUBJECTS

221. Two actively resisting individuals must be controlled.
Hit and kick the closest person.

222. Without hesitation, thrust him vigorously into the other
individual.

223. Keep moving, getting around behind the subjects using one
as a shield. Use thrusting snappy actions to put them into the van.

Avoid getting in between the two; avoid having to deal with both
of them at once. Rely on kicks for *defense*, using your hands
for *control*.

221

222

223

PRISONER CONTROL

PASSIVE RESISTANCE

224. Prisoner refuses to move. If his arms are locked and you cannot take a grip on his wrist, strike an open-hand blow onto the shoulder muscle or into the side of the neck to weaken his arm and loosen his grip.

225. Apply rear bent-arm lock.

226. Apply pressure upward on the captured arm as you grip collar or hair and lift, using wall or bars as partial support for his weight.

227. Stay well behind him as you continue to apply pressure and guide him along.

224

225

226

227

BAR GRIP RELEASE/HANDCUFF

228. Prisoner refuses to move and has tight grip on bars. Apply cuff to his right wrist, maintaining firm hold on the other cuff.

229. Buckle him down with a vigorous kick into the back of his knee.

230. With a snappy action, pull down on the cuffed wrist to bring his arm down, back and up. Apply pressure onto the bent arm as you strike his left arm or into his left elbow with vigor.

231. The combination of actions will weaken his left grip so that you can effect release and complete cuffing.

228

230

229

231

BAR GRIP/CONTROL HOLD

Prisoner grips bars and refuses to let go. Any of the following can be used to effect release.

232. Strike into the bend of the elbow or onto the forearm nerve to weaken grip.

233. Strike onto the back of the hand or wrist.

234. Grip his little finger and pull outward. This is an easy technique if you can get a hold on the little finger.

235. After effecting release of one hand, apply arm bar or variation and move him along with pressure.

232

234

233

235

PRISONER SEATED

Prisoner is sitting on the floor, gripping the bars and refusing to move. Any one of the following actions can be used to begin the sequence.

236. You can start to raise him by digging into the nerve underneath the muscle (sterno mastoid) at the side of the neck. Using your finger tips or knuckle, dig in and back.

237. Or you can dig in and up under the jaw bone with your finger tips.

238. Or you can dig in and up under the hollow behind the ear.

You could apply pressure up under the nose with the edge of your hand.

236

237

238

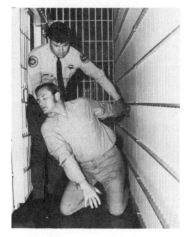 

239   240

239. When you have done one of the foregoing, maintain pressure as you grip his wrist and wheel him around away from the wall or bars.

240. Raise him by applying rear bent-arm lock and keep him moving forward for best control.

CONTROL OF PRISONERS IN CELL

To minimize danger when you enter a cell, avoid being cornered if you possibly can. Do not let the prisoner stand between you and the exit. Move him out in such a way that you go through the door first. Be prepared to cope with a weapon.

Although most cells are too small to allow two officers to enter, a backup officer or team should be close by. The team should have a plan of action before an officer enters the cell.

ONE PASSIVE, ONE ASSAULTING

241. It is immediately apparent that one of the prisoners will not give you trouble.

242. Instruct him to get out of your way by putting his hands and head on the upper bunk.

243, 244. Or order him to lie down on the bunk. Begin your control of the hostile prisoner by striking hand or foot blows to weaken and hurt him. Apply body spin.

241

242

243

244

245. Kick into the back of his knee and apply arm pressure for full control.

245

BOTH ASSAULTING

In a cell situation in which you could use one prisoner as a shield against the other, do so, subduing first one man and then the other. In the pictured situation, both prisoners confront you in a manner which does not permit you to cope with one person at a time.

246. The sequence is the same as that shown for assault by two people, the principal difference being the space limitation. Begin the defense with a kick at one person as you hit at the other man's arms, without coming into fist range of either prisoner.

247. Continue hand and foot blows, apply body spin to one man and place him between you and the other prisoner.

248. Apply arm lock of your choice and *back out* of the cell.

246

247

248

STOPPING A FIGHT

249. In this situation, one of the prisoners is obviously the assailant and the other is the victim. Do not attempt to struggle with or pull the assailant; *pushing* with a vigorous, thrusting, snappy action is more effective. Push him into the wall or against the bunk.

250. Bracing him against bunk, kick into the back of his knee as you apply the basic arm bar, smashing down onto his elbow if it is necessary.

251, 252. Keep moving. Guide him out of the cell by firm application of pressure. Or you could apply the rear bent-arm lock and back him out of the cell. Deflect the kick with a thrusting forearm parry or a two-handed slapping parry.

249

250

251

252

 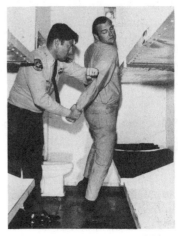

253   254

253. Kick into the knee as you slash at the side of the neck or onto the arm.

254. Apply basic arm bar, hitting vigorously onto the back of his elbow, if necessary, and pull him out of the cell. Or you could apply a rear bent-arm lock and walk him out backward.

255

PUNCHING ATTACK

255. Staying out of range of his fists, kick into the shin and slash at the arms. Repeat as necessary to weaken.

256   257

256. Apply body spin.

257. Then you could kick into the back of the knee for take-down, apply rear bent-arm lock and walk him out, or use the neck lock for control and come-along.

BLANKET FOR CONTROL

Blankets are available in most cells and are sometimes available to you in other situations where you have been warned and prepared to cope with a violent or insane person or with someone suspected of having a cutting weapon.

258. You can throw the blanket over his head.

259. You can use it to help you deflect a kick or hand blow.

258   259

260

260. You can thrust it in the face of the assailant, taking care not to smother him.

261-263. The blanket can be wound around your hand and arm for protection, especially if there is the possibility of a cutting weapon.

If a blanket is not handy you can use a pillow in a similar manner. The pillow can be thrust into the face, or used to protect your hand and arm as you parry.

If neither pillow nor blanket is available, a jacket can be used or a helmet held in front of you as a shield.

261

262

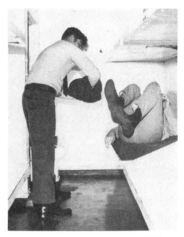

263

CONTROLLING TWO WITH BLANKET

264, 265. The situation might be that of two prisoners fighting or it could be two men refusing to be moved from the cell. Using the blanket gives you a momentary advantage.

264

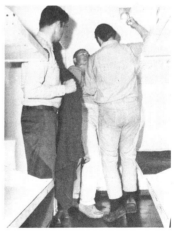

265

266   267

266. Throw the blanket over or into the face of one person.

267. Use the moment of his disorientation to kick and hit at the other individual. Immediately get behind him and move him out backward, keeping him as a shield between you and the other man.

When you have completed this portion of the course, you should be able to cope with most of the situations most of you will encounter in the daily routine.

The best way of maintaining functional skill is an occasional practice session with your partner and some mental review.

If you have a working partner, you should discuss how you will coordinate your actions in the event of various types of assault. You cannot set up the specific, exact situation as it might occur, but you can agree about a general approach. Otherwise, you might find yourselves working at cross purposes.

Whenever you are assigned a new partner, review the defense material and discuss coordinated tactics.

UNARMED DEFENSES AGAINST WEAPONS

There is little question about the appropriateness of using weapons to defend against armed attacks, but you will have more
confidence in your self-defense skill when you are not entirely
dependent on your gun. If you find yourself confronted by
an armed attack and you do *not* have access to your gun, you
should be prepared to cope with that situation. You are expected
to use *least* force in carrying out your police duties; total reliance
on your gun prevents the development of the professional skill
to use the least force necessary to do the job.

OBJECTIVES: To learn effective unarmed defenses against
attacks made with rigid striking weapons (bludgeon, tire-iron,
etc.), flexible weapons (chain, belt, etc.) and cutting weapons.
To learn preventive procedure to prevent gun drawing. To learn
the essential difference between gun threat and any other assault.
To learn the actions of different types of guns in order to prevent
firing. To learn procedures of safe practice of weapons defenses.

DEFENSES AGAINST BLUDGEON

Any rigid striking weapon, such as club, stick, tire iron, pipe or
similar bludgeon presents a unique situation--one in which your
area of safety is in close to the assailant, rather than out of his
fist range. When he holds a bludgeon it extends his hitting
distance; when you are in very close he cannot effectively use
this type of weapon. *Do not attempt to block or grab the weapon.* Do not take the weapon away from the assailant until you
have subdued him.

268. Against a back-handed
swinging attack, step in and
to the outside of the striking
arm and block the arm, not
the weapon, with a single or
double forearm blow. Kick
into the knee, if necessary.

268

269   270

269. Apply arm bar, hitting down onto his elbow vigorously
to make him release the weapon. You can then put him on the
ground or walk him away.

WIDE ARC ATTACK

270. Against a wide swinging blow, step in close and block the
hitting arm.

271. With one hand, grip the striking arm and lock it outward
as you hit and kick to weaken him.

272. You can then take him down or apply control hold for
come-along.

THRUST ATTACK

273. Against a thrusting attack or an overhead attack, side-step
and deflect the striking arm with a back-handed forearm blow.

274. Grip his wrist, not the weapon, and thrust it away from you
as you kick into the knee.

275. Apply arm bar, striking down onto his elbow with force,
if necessary. Use additional kicks, if necessary. At this point you
can put him on the ground or apply control hold for come-along.

271

272

273

274

275

276   277

KNIFE THREAT

A cool head and a calm exterior are your most useful defense aids in such a situation. Do not shout, threaten or bluster.

Your primary purpose is to engage his attention for a precious second--diverting him for the brief time required to begin your defense. You must not make sudden or dramatic gestures or movements; your distraction should be subtle. It may take the form of a low-voiced conversation, slight foot movement, slight head movement, or . . .

276. a slight finger-wiggling gesture to which he will turn his eyes.

277. With a forceful cross-body thrust, deflect his knife hand away from your body. Lock your arm outward to immobilize his arm.

Do not attempt to grip or grapple with the knife. Do not attempt to take the knife away until you have subdued the assailant.

If you try to grab the knife hand or block the knife itself, you are in greatest danger of being cut. The man who carries a knife is likely to be adept at using it; you would have to be lightning-fast to grip his hand and avoid being cut. In any confrontation with an armed person there is some danger of injury, but these defenses minimize that possibility.

278   279

278. Finger stabs into the eyes or throat might be appropriate and necessary.

279. Kick forcefully into the knee as you twist his wrist with both your hands. Continue kicking until he is subdued.

280   281

280. The attack style is high, overhead.

281. The attack style is low, thrusting. In either case the defense is similar. In both instances you have space in which to move away. Step out to the side of the attacking arm and parry his arm, not the knife, with a forceful forearm blow.

282

283

282. Kick into the knee.

283. Grip his arm and lock your arms outward as you continue to kick until he is subdued. Even though he may be strong, the locking action of your arms can prevent his reaching you with the knife while you are subduing him with vigorous kicks.

KNIFE DEFENSES: WITH CHAIR, JACKET, BLANKET

Against an assailant armed with a knife or sharp cutting weapon, kicking is the best defense. It is ineffective and dangerous to attempt to grip or grapple with the knife or knife hand. If you are forewarned and prepared to cope with the situation, try to use a chair, jacket or blanket to give you added protection.

284

285

284. Approach the knife-armed individual with the chair held in an obviously protective manner. If there is any possibility of talking him into submission, do not present yourself as vulnerable or threatening.

285. If necessary, you can kick without getting into cutting range. Kick until he is hurt. Do not attempt to get in close for disarming and control until he has been hurt and weakened.

286   287

286. Wind the jacket around your hand and wrist.

287. Use a back-handed parry to deflect his knife hand as you kick with vigor to start the defense.

288. With a blanket you can cover and tangle the knife hand as you kick.

Do not attempt to remove the weapon until you have subdued him with kicks.

288

289   290

FLEXIBLE WEAPONS: CHAIN, ROPE, SAP, BELT, ETC.

The untrained, automatic response to the threat of attack with
a flexible weapon is drawing back and/or trying to grab the
weapon. Merely drawing back places you in an even more vulnerable position to be hit; trying to grab a swinging flexible
weapon is not efficient. There are two relatively safe areas--
in close or completely out of range.

289. The intent to use a flexible weapon is easily read.

290. If you are already in close, move in quickly as the attack
is signalled and block his arm as you kick and hit. Do not attempt
to take away his weapon until you have subdued him and have
him under control.

291. If you are not in close, jump a step completely out of range
of the swinging object.

292. After his swinging arm has gone by, grip it with both your
hands and lock your arms outward as you kick until he is subdued.

291

292

293

PREVENTING WEAPON DRAWING

This is a practice procedure to learn a fast, simple, effective response to the gesture which might mean that the suspect is drawing a gun.

293. Do not wait for the weapon to be fully drawn to respond. As his hand goes to his side, grip his arm with your left hand and clamp down onto his hand with your right hand, pushing his hand and his weapon into his side.

Practice this tactic for speed of response to the reaching gesture. Practice on both sides. Partners should practice this with unloaded guns. (Both partners check to make certain guns are not loaded.)

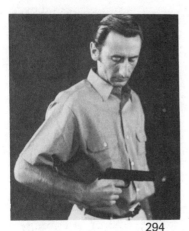

294   295

UNARMED DEFENSE AGAINST GUNS

It is essential to understand how to stop the action of a gun
before you attempt defenses against gun attack. Old style
jujitsu and aikido gun defenses which treat guns as though they
were metal swords are not appropriate. The old style of training
is based on the false assumption that you can learn to move your
hands faster than your opponent can pull a trigger. Gun defenses,
to be effective, must be realistic; a gun is not a metal stick and
a trigger can be pulled in a split second. The "lightning speed"
which the old style defenses rely upon cannot be achieved by
most individuals.

294. The semi-automatic handgun with a hammer is activated
by pulling back the slide, which cocks the hammer. You can prevent the firing of this gun by clamping down on the hammer.

295. The revolver mechanism can be stopped by clamping down
on the hammer or, in the case of double-action, by clamping
down on the cylinder.

296. A hammerless handgun first
shot cannot be prevented. A
second shot can be prevented by
clamping down over the slide,
preventing ejection.

296

297

A major factor in effective gun defense is the use of a single hand
motion to produce two essential results: deflection of the gun
barrel away from you and hindering the action of the mechanism.

To produce these results, it is necessary to grip the weapon itself
rather than the gun hand. Unlike the situation of knife attack in
which it is safer to avoid gripping or grappling with the cutting
weapon, the safe procedure in gun defenses is to grip the gun.
Gripping the weapon reduces the risk of lethal injury, but it
does involve the minor risk of hurting your hand. A powder burn
or cut on your hand is far less serious than a bullet in your body.

FOR SAFETY IN PRACTICE of gun defense, *both* partners
always check the gun to make sure it is not loaded. Practice
clamping the gun and deflecting the barrel as a single action.

297. The gun is drawn. Clamp your hand over the gun to stop
its action as you thrust his hand and the gun barrel away from
you. Do this portion of the defense slowly a few times until you
do it correctly. Practice on both sides. Continue to practice,
increasing the speed of your action as you develop skill. As you
deflect, twist your body out of the danger zone (as shown) and
twist his wrist sharply for additional protection.

There is a type of toy gun which works well for practice. It
shoots a rubber-tipped dart. The partner shooting the toy gun
will try to hit you with the blunt dart. Even though he knows
what you are going to do, which an actual assailant would not,
you will find that you can develop the skill to deflect the gun
with moderate practice.

After learning the foregoing portion of the gun defense, you are
ready to practice the entire sequence.

298   299

CLOSE-IN THREAT: BASIC TACTICS

298. Obviously, this type of gun defense can only be applied to
a threatened attack where you are within arms' reach. Your
judgment is the guide to action in such a situation. If you decide
that you have only one of two choices--to be shot or to attempt
the defense--you have nothing to lose in the attempt. In fact,
if his only intention is to shoot you, you are less vulnerable as
a moving target than if you are passive.

299. Use a *subtle* distracting action. Anything you do to divert
his attention for a fraction of a moment is a precious advantage
for you. Slight finger-wiggling, whispering, hand-moving or
eye-shifting might be useful. Or he may provide the proper
moment for your first action by talking, turning his head or
reaching toward you.

300. Thrust your hand cross-body onto the weapon, clamping
the mechanism and twisting his wrist away from you, moving
your body as you thrust. Lock your arm rigidly to immobilize
his arm for a moment.

301. Finger stabs into his eyes.

300

301

302

303

302. Vigorous kicks into the knee. Repeat these two actions, alternating high and low blows until he is hurt.

303. Only after you have hurt him do you grip his gun with both your hands (maintaining the stop-mechanism grip) and twist it out of his hand.

304   305

An alternate ending may be used. It is a matter of individual preference. Either ending is "good," but the one which suits you better is the one which you should practice.

304. After hurting, weakening and disorienting him, grip the gun (maintaining the stop-mechanism grip) and pull his arm sharply forward so that the gun and gun hand go past your body.

305. Clamp your forearm over his upper arm as you twist his wrist sharply and disarm.

GUN AT HIP

This defense is more difficult than the foregoing gun defense. Fast, well-timed movements would be essential for effective use.

306. You decide that you must attempt the defense. Obviously you must be in fairly close.

307. Distract, using a subtle gesture, or talk to him to shift his attention.

308. With a snappy action, thrust your hand forward to twist and push the gun barrel against his body, clamping the mechanism to stop its action. Quickly follow with finger stabs into the eyes.

309. Without hesitation, continue by kicking with vigor into the knee and grip the gun with both hands to lock it into his body.

306

307

308

309

310. When forceful kicks have hurt him, twist his wrist sharply (maintaining the stop-mechanism hold) and disarm.

310

311

312

GUN AT BACK

311. The gun is held at your back. If you can, glance around to see which hand holds the gun--most people are right-handed.

312. Make a slight, subtle distracting movement.

313. With a sharp, slashing forearm blow, hit his arm away to divert the gun barrel from your body.

314. Grip the gun, stopping the action of the mechanism. Extend your arm rigidly to lock his arm away from you as you use finger stabs into the eyes.

315. Grip his arm with both your arms as you kick vigorously into the knee, repeating as necessary to hurt him.

316. Turning clockwise, clamp your elbow over his upper arm as you twist his wrist sharply to disarm.

313

314

315

316

317

318

319

320

GUN AT HEAD

317. With the gun held at your head, there is little likelihood of being able to see which hand holds the gun. Assume it is the right hand. Distract.

318. Turn sharply as you duck down and slash at his arm to divert the gun barrel away from you.

319. Grip the gun to stop the mechanism as you kick into the knee, continuing as necessary to hurt and subdue him.

320. Twist his wrist sharply with your right hand as you disarm with your left hand, or from the action shown in 319 you can apply the ending shown in 316. Try both endings and practice the one which is more comfortable for you.

321

322

323

DEFENSE AGAINST RIFLE OR SHOTGUN

321. The long-barrelled gun is held within arm's reach. Distract.

322. Using your left hand for a parrying action, thrust the barrel cross-body, away from you.

323. Clamp your left hand over his gun hand to hamper his use of it and to prevent his using a butt stroke against you. With your right hand, grip the forward stock, as shown. Lock both arms rigidly outward as you kick vigorously into the knee. Continue kicking until you have hurt him.

324

325

324. When he has been hurt, twist the weapon counterclockwise past his head, over his shoulder.

325. Using your forward body motion to assist you, use snappy arm action to release the weapon. Follow through with arm and body action, taking a step in the direction in which you are releasing the gun to insure completion of disarming.

326

327

AT BACK

326. If the weapon is held at your back, assume it is held in the right hand unless you can glance back. Distract.

327. With a snappy slashing blow, divert the barrel away from you as you turn around. Continue in the same way as described in 323-325.

BATON TECHNIQUES

OBJECTIVES: To learn appropriate applications of baton
tactics for police defense and control. To evaluate types of
baton weapons. To learn use of the baton with least show of
force. To learn basic techniques and baton striking methods.
To evaluate body targets for baton blows to minimize possibility of injury. To learn control holds applied with aid of
baton. To demonstrate solo practice routines for development
of skill and flexibility.

THE MIDDLE FORCE

The officer who has appropriate and adequate training and the
right temperament for modern police work will be able to
distinguish four principal levels of authority and control. They
range from the use of no force (persuasion and negotiation) to
minimum force (weaponless techniques) to middle force (baton
techniques) to maximum force (firearms).

The valuable middle range of control techniques and tactics is
not used to its fullest potential because officers have not been
given appropriate or adequate instruction in the effective use
of the baton.

To counteract the public impression of brutal cops swinging
their nightsticks at innocent citizens, some departments have
adapted methods of "defensive" baton tactics and have launched
publicity campaigns to improve their "image." When experience
convinces them that the beautiful aikido-like tactics are practical
only for highly trained individuals, they may decide that it is
best not to rely on the baton, or may adopt needlessly forceful
tactics to insure personal safety. Or they may publicize one
style of baton training while training their officers in a totally
different style.

When an officer has confidence in *all* of his resources--persuasion,
weaponless tactics, baton techniques, firearms--there is less
likelihood of unnecessary force being used.

In a professional environment and with good leadership at all
levels of command, officers will increasingly learn to respond
with appropriate defense, control, and rescue tactics--trying
negotiation if at all possible, attempting weaponless defense if
it is feasible, using the baton if it is appropriate, and resorting to
firearms if no other resource insures both safety and success.

TEACHING METHOD

The single greatest impediment to teaching and learning police
baton work is the old fashioned by-the-numbers approach. Baton
tactics are still widely taught as though for massed confrontation
in formation. This method resembles close-order drill and may
have some value for disciplined, coordinated group action, but
it is next to useless for an officer on the job in the street.

For most of the situations which the officer encounters, there is
no field commander and no formation. When coordinated,
disciplined group action is anticipated as a real need, then drill
training is appropriate. For most street encounters, the officer
needs self-control, good judgment and flexibility of response
rather than mechanical reactions.

GROMMET OR THONG?

Most departments use a baton with a thong or a baton with a
rubber or plastic grommet. There are advantages and disadvantages to each style. When the alternatives are limited to *either*
a thong or a grommet, choices are made largely on the basis of
personal preference.

THE GROMMET

Wearing a stick with a grommet, the officer presents a neat
appearance. The grommet allows a firm grip to be taken, a grip
which can be maintained if the stick is grabbed and twisted.
The grommet-held stick can be drawn easily and quickly, unless
the grommet acts as a stopper in the ring.

The major disadvantage of the grommet-held stick is that it
must be held in one hand or under the arm when it is not in the
ring. Unless the stick is being used in conjunction with a control
hold, this severely limits the officer's movements. After it has
been used for defense or to subdue an assaulting or resisting
individual, the grommet-held stick must then be put back into
the ring, held under the arm or in the hand, or it must be put
down. Putting the stick down is dangerous. Putting the stick
back in the ring while trying to maintain control of a subject is
difficult. Holding the stick under the arm makes it awkward to
apply handcuffs; holding the stick in one hand makes it almost
impossible.

Unable to disengage the stick easily while moving to the next
step of handcuffing, walking and securing the person, the officer
may be tempted to use unnecessary force--just to make sure!

Theoretically, the grommet allows a quick draw from the ring. In practice, the grommet may act as a stopper, preventing the draw, if the narrow end of the grommet enters the ring first and is wedged in.

THE THONG

Arguments against the use of a thong-held baton are: A secure manner of wearing the baton prevents quick draw; if the stick is gripped and pulled, the officer's wrist can be hurt; the stick is weakened by drilling or grooving to attach the thong.

The argument that the officer can be hurt (if the thong-held stick is wrestled away from him) is based on an improper and inefficient method of looping the thong. When it is held correctly (as shown in photos 328-330) the thong-held baton offers the officer the most flexibility and security, the best chances of maintaining a grip on the stick, and the best chance of avoiding injury if the stick is snapped or jerked away.

If the thong hold (or groove) is put between the hand grip area and the butt of the stick, there is no strain on the striking portion of the baton.

The thong allows easy disengagement of the stick after it has been used and it does not limit actions to the same degree that the grommet-held stick does. With the thong looped over the thumb, as shown in the instruction which follows, the officer can use both hands. Though the stick is dangling, it is less of an impediment to movement than would be a hand-held stick or a stick under the arm.

THE ALTERNATIVE

It is my view that there is an alternative to the either/or proposition. Maximum security and efficiency can be achieved by using a baton which has both grommet and thong.

Reviewing all of the arguments for and against grommet and thong, it seems clear that the advantages of each should be utilized. The grommet-and-thong-held stick affords the greatest amount of safety and security. It is the most flexible in use, allowing for individual style and preference of the officer in tactical application.

In photos 328-330 the grommet-and-thong baton is shown; to eliminate the stopper-like effect of wedging the grommet into the ring, the grommet has been turned so that the wide end enters the ring first.

There are departments which use this or a similar thong-and-grommet baton. In practice it has demonstrated safety features and tactical superiority over thong-only or grommet-only sticks.

Although I favor the grommet-and-thong baton, I have selected techniques which can be adapted, for the most part, to all of the various kinds of sticks which are used by law enforcement agencies throughout the world. The techniques are demonstrated by an officer using his department's standard baton--a 26-inch stick with a grommet.

LOOPING THE THONG: CORRECT PROCEDURE

328. Holding the stick with your left hand, loop the thong around your right thumb and across the back of your hand.

329. Turn your hand over, ready to grip the stick. The thong should be long enough so that it is not too tight over the back of your hand, but there should be no slack. Each officer will require an individual adjustment.

330. Gripping the baton in this fashion, you have maximum grip security and maximum ease of release if necessary.

KEEPING A LOW PROFILE

You can be on guard, ready to use the baton as necessary, without brandishing the stick. You can be prepared to put the stick into action without losing your negotiating power if you maintain a neutral stance.

331. The stick is drawn and the officer is alert and ready. Holding the stick down and behind his leg does not conceal it, but it has a considerably cooler effect than a display of the weapon. A well-balanced stance gives added strength and authority to this low-profile, guarded position.

332. The stick is not drawn but is held horizontally for quick drawing if necessary. The position of the hands partly conceals the weapon but it is obvious that it could be drawn and used.

333. Midway between a neutral stance and a threatening posture is this well-guarded ready stance. Keep an appropriately safe distance from the subject. The baton is visible but not threatening. The other hand is held in a ready guard position. Your feet are about shoulder-width apart with your weight distributed equally on both. You should be ready to advance, retreat or move to the side without hesitation. Make eye contact and be alert for the first move which would signal the need for putting the stick into action.

328

329

330

331

332

333

334

335

ONE-HAND SNAP BLOW

The manner of holding the baton for the one-hand snap blow
will vary according to preference and according to the construc-
tion of the stick. If there is a rubber grommet, the strongest
grip is with the thumb and forefinger gripping the grommet.
There are those who prefer a hold with the thumb extended
along the stick because they feel that it gives them a greater
degree of control. The disadvantage of the extended-thumb grip
is that it creates an area of weakness in the grip at the space
between the thumb and forefinger. My preference is for the
stronger grip with the thumb overlapping the forefinger. If the
stick does not have a grommet, take a firm grip at the serrated
section.

The snap blow is a quick, whipping action with recoil. It is not
a pounding or smashing blow. The main action is in the wrist.

334. A backhand snap blow into the side of the neck.

335. A forehand snap blow into the side of the neck.

336. Avoid moving in closer than you need to to use your baton.
In this representation the officer has shifted his head into
hitting range of the subject.

337. Here he shows control and positive reaction without
putting himself into a vulnerable position.

AVOID THIS   336

337

AVOID THIS   338

339

338. Avoid this error. In this representation the officer has nullified his advantage by bending down. His head is within reach of the subject's hands. He is in relatively poor balance.

339. Use your baton to the best advantage. One of the principle virtues of your stick weapon is that you can strike from a safe distance.

340   341

340. A downward snap blow onto the shoulder muscle.

341. A downward snap blow onto the tip of the shoulder.

342. A downward snap blow into the bend of the elbow or onto the mound of the forearm.

343, 344. A downward snap onto the wrist, back of hand or onto the knuckles.

345. An upward snap blow can be delivered against the elbow, as shown, or up under the forearm or wrist as a deflecting action.

342   343

344

345

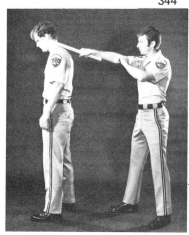

346

347

346. Downward snap blow onto the shoulder muscle.

347. Forward snap blow at the shoulder blade.

348. Backhand snap at the upper arm.

348

349   350

349. Backhand snap at the elbow joint.

350, 351. If the target of opportunity is the leg, you can deliver a snap blow into the back of the knee or into the calf.

352. If the leg is the target of opportunity, you can strike a snap blow into the side of the knee . . .

353. or the shin . . .

354. or the ankle.

351   352

353

354

355

356

BLOCKING WITH A SNAP BLOW

355, 356. The one-hand snap blow can be used effectively for blocking fist blows. You can move swiftly to block one punching or reaching hand and then the other, if necessary. Blocking can be done safely out of hitting range of the assailant.

357

ONE-HAND FORWARD JAB

357. The forward thrust is directed straight to the midsection. See page 164 for an explanation of the risk of injury if the jabbing thrust is directed upward.

358   359

TWO-HAND GRIP

358. The stick is held about three inches from each end. A right-handed person would grip as shown, the right hand palm down and the left hand palm up.

359. The stick can be employed to thrust and push . . .

360

361

362

363

360. to strike . . .

361-363. and to block blows.

364

SLIP-THRUST

Although this technique has limited value, it is useful and it can be applied without swinging the stick.

364. Holding the baton point forward, you can maintain a posture which does not necessarily mean that you intend to use physical action.

365, 366. If the subject makes a threatening move, a quick slide-and-recovery blow can be applied. The photo shows the blow directed up under the jaw. Other targets of opportunity might be into the side of the neck, at the shoulder muscle or against a moving hand or arm.

TENSION BLOWS

367. Holding the baton with both hands, as shown, you are in a guarded posture from which you can negotiate and which does not commit you to physical action. Holding the stick about three inches from each end, your right hand grips palm down and your left hand grips palm up. Tension is created by pulling back with your left hand as you push forward with your right hand.

368. At the instant a hostile or threatening move is made, you strike with a quick release of the spring tension.

A similar circumstance would be one in which the baton is being held under your arm while you use your hands for making notes or writing a citation. At the first indication of aggressive action, pull and hit.

369. The baton is under your arm with the butt end forward. There are circumstances in which you might be in this position if your baton does not have a thong.

370. At the cue of "attack" slide the baton forward and without hesitation hit downward with the point.

Tension is developed by pulling down with your hand; when the stick is released, it snaps forward.

365

366

367

368

369

370

371

372

373

374

QUICK RESPONSE/LOW PROFILE

371. When you hold the stick at your side you convey a neutral image. Even though the stick is drawn, you are in a favorable negotiating position. If you keep a suitable distance between you and the subject and if you are alert to his movements, you can be ready to go into action, if necessary, while having the advantage of maintaining a non-threatening stance which gives you leeway time during which you might establish verbal control.

At the first sign of hostile action you are ready to strike in a variety of ways.

372. Using the butt end of the baton straight forward.

373, 374. Using an upward snap thrust, hitting with the point.

375

376

375. Using a backhand circular snap into the side of the neck.

376. Using a forward jab, striking with the butt.

377

378

MID-GRIP BLOWS

Although the mid-grip method of striking is not the most flexible or practical, you should know how to use the stick if you have picked it up this way in a hurry, in an emergency, or if you happen to be holding it in this manner.

377. You can strike downward with the point.

378. You can snap up, using the butt as the striking point.

379   380

379, 380. You can use either the point or the butt end in a jabbing fashion.

TWO-HAND SNAP

Holding your stick weapon with both hands gives high visibility to your actions. You would use this technique against a cutting or hitting weapon, against an adversary considerably larger than yourself or against an extremely violent individual. By holding the baton in both hands you increase the force of the blow you can deliver while staying well out of range of a knife, pipe, reaching or punching arms or a kicking leg. The partner shown left uses his baton to represent the weapon of attack.

Although your stick is being held with both hands, avoid using it as a bat. The movements are snappy, the hitting arc is small. Keep your eyes on the attacking weapon (or hands or feet) and on the point of your baton.

381. The ready stance, a highly visible guard.

382. As the attacking weapon comes forward, block it with a snappy forceful blow . . .

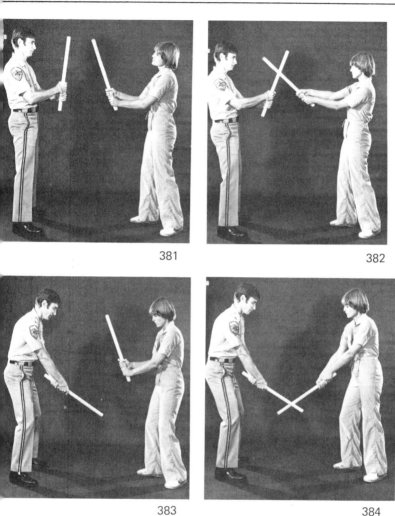

381

382

383

384

383. and as your partner lowers the attacking weapon, draw your stick back up and over in a short, circular movement . . .

384. to hit the other side of the attacking weapon.

Practice this technique using backhand and forehand blows against high and low attack points.

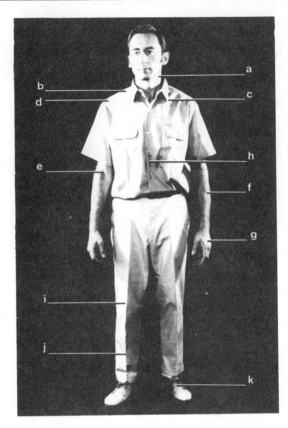

385

STRIKING AREAS

Appropriate body target areas for baton blows will vary according to circumstances. The effects of a baton blow--pain, immobilization, possible risk of injury--will be different in different situations. The force of the blow, the area struck, the health, fitness, frame and pain tolerance of the subject are some of the factors which will govern the result.

A stick weapon delivers greater force than a bare hand blow. The striking areas for baton work are not always the same as for weaponless defense.

The descriptions of the possible effects of baton blows can only be approximate. You must realize that any sufficiently forceful blow made with a stick weapon against *any* part of the body could deliver enough impact to fracture bones, refer transmitted force to the internal organs, or sever veins or arteries. A baton blow against a frail or vulnerable person could result in serious or permanent injury. If you must control or immobilize a very small or frail individual, be aware of the risk of forceful blows.

FRONT: PHOTO 385

a. SIDE OF THE NECK: The side of the neck is often a suitable target of opportunity, even when it is partially protected by clothing. A backhand or forehand snap blow into the side of the neck is an effective tactic. A moderately forceful blow can cause extreme pain; a forceful blow could result in temporary paralysis or unconsciousness.

b. SHOULDER MUSCLE: The shoulder muscle extends from the base of the side of the neck almost to the tip of the shoulder. A moderately forceful downward snap blow onto the shoulder muscle causes pain and numbness. It might immobilize the arm for a short time and might result in muscle spasm. A heavy blow could injure muscle, ligaments and tendons. The objective of hitting at the shoulder muscle is to cause distracting pain and temporary immobility.

c. CLAVICLE (collar bone): The objective of hitting the clavicle with a stick weapon is to break it. Against a gun or knife-armed individual, striking a forceful blow to the clavicle would be justified in most instances. (If breaking a bone is needless force in subduing the subject, you will harm your case.) The clavicle is an all-or-nothing target. If it is not broken, the violent subject is fully capable of action. If it is broken, arm movement is severely limited.

My preference is the shoulder muscle as a target. If you strike forcefully at the shoulder muscle, you need not break a bone or inflict serious, permanent injury to accomplish the objective of hurting and distracting the subject for the brief period necessary to handcuff and secure him.

d. TIP OF THE SHOULDER: A downward snap onto the tip of the shoulder causes pain and could numb the arm. A heavy blow might chip bone or result in joint separation.

e. ELBOW (inside): Striking at the inside of the elbow joint can bend the arm, cause pain and numb. A forceful blow can injure.

f. FOREARM: The mound of the forearm is an excellent, low-risk-of-injury target area. It can be struck while you are well out of hitting or grabbing range. A snappy blow onto the forearm muscle will deflect, hurt and probably numb the arm.

g. WRIST/HAND/KNUCKLES/FINGERS: Against a moving
or reaching hand, a blow struck at the wrist, back of hand, or
knuckles or fingers is effective. The target area is broad enough to
allow a degree of flexibility; exact pin-point accuracy is not
required. Any part of the area which is struck will divert,
deflect and hurt the hand or wrist. Against a hand reaching for
a weapon or hurling object, a quick, snappy baton blow against
the wrist or hand could prevent the completion of the assault.

h. MID-BODY: A jabbing, straight-in thrust into the mid-body
will cause considerable pain and could result in loss of breath.
If a straight-in blow is used, considerable force would cause
internal injury.

If the baton blow is struck in an upward direction, there is a
significant increase in the risk of injury. An upward blow will
deliver direct or referred impact to the vital organs--liver, lungs
and heart--and might cause serious, irreversible injury, or if
sufficiently forceful, could be fatal.

Vomiting might occur after a moderate or a forceful blow
straight-in or upward. Persistent vomiting with blood is a
possible symptom of internal injury. If it occurs, the individual
should be given medical attention as soon as possible.

i. KNEE: A moderately forceful blow into the front of the knee
causes pain and could result in bone bruise. A heavy blow might
dislodge the kneecap and immobilize the subject. A blow into
the side of the knee causes pain. A forceful blow could injure
the ligaments and could incapacitate the subject.

j. SHIN: The shin is particularly sensitive to pain on most
people. Unless the individual is unresponsive to pain sensation
because of an emotional state or is drunk or otherwise drugged,
a snappy, moderately forceful blow will hurt enough to divert
attention.

k. ANKLE/FOOT: A snappy blow against the ankle bone causes
distracting pain. A forceful blow could crack one of the many
small bones in the foot and ankle and could immobilize the
subject.

When appropriate to the situation, the point or the butt of the
baton can be used to nudge and push. This action is not a blow;
it is simply pressure used to assist an action such as walking a
suspect or moving an unresponsive individual. The appropriate
body areas for nudging are the armpit, under the last rib, the
mid-body and the small of the back.

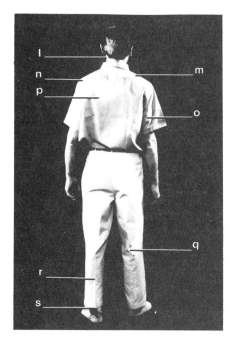

BACK: PHOTO 386

l. SIDE OF NECK

m. SHOULDER MUSCLE

n. TIP OF SHOULDER

o. BACK OF UPPER ARM: Striking into the back of the upper arm is a low-risk-of-injury tactic which can numb and temporarily incapacitate the arm.

p. UNDER THE SHOULDER BLADE: Directly under the shoulder blade is a muscle area which, if struck, may go into spasm, incapacitating the individual for a short time.

q. KNEE: Striking into the back of the knee causes pain; a snappy, forceful blow can put the individual on the ground.

r. CALF: Striking into the calf can result in muscle spasm, which is temporarily incapacitating.

s. TENDON/ANKLE: A blow at the lower leg could hit the tendon or ankle bone. If the tendon is struck, it could briefly incapacitate; if it is struck with considerable force, it could injure the tendon. Striking the ankle bone causes pain.

As pointed out earlier, the factors which affect the selection of target areas and the degree of force used are suitability and opportunity. It is my opinion that *kicking* into the leg of an assailant is more likely to be practical than striking at the leg with a baton. Your department may have a bias against using foot blows and in that event you would be advised to use baton tactics.

Unless grave and unusual danger is presented by an extremely violent individual, the high-risk-of-injury body areas will be avoided by ethical, professional, well-trained officers. Whenever a person can be prevented from assaulting or can be controlled without resorting to high-risk-of-injury tactics, striking at high risk, vulnerable body areas is needless force.

The high risk, vulnerable areas are head, windpipe, mouth, cardiac notch, spleen, kidney, base of the skull, 7th vertebra and coccyx.

Any forceful blow to the head is potentially dangerous because of referred impact against the skull. Even a moderately forceful blow to the windpipe can cause serious injury; a broken windpipe is fatal unless tracheotomy follows immediately. Hitting into the mouth with a stick weapon is almost certain to break teeth. As noted earlier, a blow into the cardiac notch involves high risk of damage to vital organs and is potentially fatal. The spleen and the kidney are easily damaged; a moderately forceful stick blow can inflict serious injury. Forceful stick weapon blows against the base of the skull could be fatal. If the 7th vertebra is struck with force, there is a likelihood of serious, permanent injury. Permanent disability is possible if a heavy blow is struck against the coccyx.

It is my view that baton design should include built-in safeguards against lethal blows. A baton which will not break if it is used with extreme force is not appropriate for everyday police work. For use as a battering ram, for delivering great force, a separate baton should be used. The argument is made that in England a truncheon is used which is capable of delivering more forceful blows than the commonly used United States types of police batons. In England there are legal limits and clear definitions of truncheon tactics which are permitted and those which are prohibited. Because we have no generally accepted standards and no clear definitions of acceptable baton tactics, a greater measure of preventive safety is called for in the design and structure of the police stick weapon.

QUICK DRAW & STRIKING PRACTICE

Quick draw practice is essential. When you are confident of your ability to respond quickly and effectively you are less likely to draw the stick prematurely and you are less likely to over-react.

You can move from lesser to greater force if the situation calls for it. It is very difficult to reduce the use of force once it is started. Keep your hands away from your stick unless you think you will need to draw it. When it is drawn, do not brandish or swing it unless you are using it. The cooling-down cop knows that many situations can be controlled by calming actions which do not threaten or challenge the potentially violent individual. If you can avoid touching the stick until you decide to use it and have the ability to put it into action quickly and efficiently you extend your negotiating options.

The procedures which follow will introduce you to six ways of drawing and hitting. Practice all of the illustrated quick draws and then select the two or three which suit your style of movement and which feel right for you. Practice those until you can use them quickly and effectively.

QUICK DRAW NO. 1

387. Your practice partner holds his baton in place as a target. Begin from a well balanced, completely neutral posture, both hands at your sides. Make eye contact.

388. As your partner cues the "attack" by moving his baton slightly, grasp the butt of your stick weapon and without hesitation . . .

387 388

389

390

391

389. snap upward to hit the target with the point . . .

390. and immediately grasp the stick with your left hand as it recoils and . . .

391. deliver a second blow downward with the butt end.

392   393

394   395

QUICK DRAW NO. 2

392. Your practice partner holds his baton point up to simulate
a target. Facing him in a well balanced, neutral stance, you draw
your stick weapon at his cue of "attack"--a slight movement of
his baton . . .

393. and without hesitation, deliver a backhand snap blow . . .

394. and draw the stick back . . .

395. to deliver a forehand snap blow to the other side of the
attacking target. The transition movement between the first
and second blows should be a small arc.

396

397

398

QUICK DRAW NO. 3

396. At your partner's signal of "attack" you draw your stick and strike with the butt end . . .

397. and without hesitation, grip the point end with your left hand . . .

398. and deliver an upward thrust with the point . . .

followed by a downward snap with the butt (no photo).

399

400

401

402

QUICK DRAW NO. 4

399. The baton is under your arm.

400. At the cue of "attack" you draw the stick and . . .

401. snap upward against the wrist or hand . . .

402. and without hesitation, deliver a second downward snap onto the back of the hand or wrist.

403

404

405

406

QUICK DRAW NO. 5

403. At the cue of "attack" you draw the baton with your left hand holding the butt end . . .

404. and strike straight forward with the butt . . .

405. and without hesitation you grip the point end with your right hand and . . .

406. deliver an upward blow with the point . . .

407. followed immediately by a downward blow with the butt.

407

408

409

410

QUICK DRAW NO. 6

408. The baton is drawn with your left hand and you deliver an upward blow with the point . . .

409. and without hesitation you grip with your right hand and . . .

410. deliver a downward blow with the butt.

411

412

413

414

RELEASING THE GRIPPED STICK: NO. 1

411, 412. Pull the grabbed stick toward yourself as you kick into the knee or shin. His upper body comes forward and he reacts to your pull by pulling back.

413-415. Go with his pulling action and strike into the target of opportunity and then snap the stick down and away. Strike again if necessary to effect control.

RELEASING THE GRIPPED STICK: NO. 2

416. Kick into the knee or shin and step toward his side as you raise the grabbed stick, 417, roll it over his shoulder, 418, and move around behind him and snap the stick free, 419.

420. Strike into an appropriate available target if necessary to apply the control technique.

415

416

417

418

419

420

RELEASING THE GRIPPED STICK: NO. 3

421. The stick is grabbed.

422. As you step forward with your right foot and put body thrust into your action, twist the stick with a snappy movement, raising with your right hand and lowering with your left hand . . .

423. and without hesitation step toward his side as you reverse the twisting action, down and toward yourself with your right hand and up, over and down with your left hand.

Follow through as you walk around behind him and roll the stick over his shoulder with your left hand. Strike an appropriate target, if necessary, and apply a control hold (no photo).

CONTROL HOLDS WITH BATON

Knowing how to apply control holds with the baton gives you flexibility in the choice of tactics. Using the baton as part of a control hold solves some of the problems which arise if your stick weapon does not have a thong. You need only know a few baton holding techniques for practical application, but you should be able to use the few you know quickly and efficiently, which means that you will have to practice these techniques in order to maintain functional skill. The holds which follow are easy to learn and skill can be maintained with relatively little practice.

ARM BAR/BATON

424. The action in this technique is similar to the basic arm bar. But where the weaponless arm bar is started by gripping the person's wrist with your right hand, the arm bar with baton starts with a blow onto the forearm and a simultaneous gripping of the wrist with your left hand.

425. Without hesitation, twist the wrist to turn the elbow joint up. Apply pressure down on the elbow as you pull up on the captured wrist.

Note that the stick is placed in such a manner that downward pressure is made with your hand and arm. If you place the stick so that your hand is as close as possible to the elbow joint, you will have maximum efficiency. From this position you can walk the subject or put him on the ground.

421

422

423

424

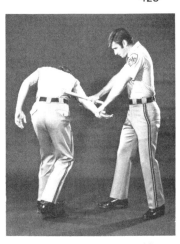

425

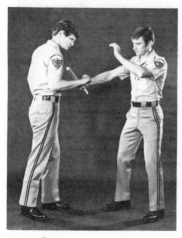 

426   427

REAR BENT-ARM LOCK/BATON

426. Strike at the reaching hand or wrist and . . .

427. grip the wrist with your left hand as you hit onto the forearm muscle and . . .

428. roll the baton across his arm (away from you) as you begin to twist his arm down and back . . .

429. and up, as you move around behind him and position the baton under his arm and over yours, as shown. Pressure can be applied by levering your elbow out and up as you pull back on his collar or hair to walk him, or . . .

430. push down on his head to put him on the ground.

431. Or you can maintain pressure with your left arm, freeing your right hand to reach for the handcuffs.

ARM TWIST WITH NECK LEVER/BATON

432. Strike at the hand or wrist and . . .

433. grip the hand with your left hand as you . . .

428

429

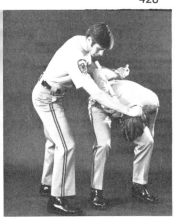

430

431

432

433

434. move around behind him, maintaining your grip to twist his arm as you move, and begin to slide the baton . . .

435. up his captured arm and press it against the back of his neck. If you push forward with your right arm extended and pull his twisted arm back, you will have enough control to allow you to walk the subject, or, if appropriate, put him onto his knees or onto the ground.

QUICK DRAW & ARM TWIST

Although any technique of baton defense and/or control might start with a quick drawing of your stick weapon, the quick draw-and-strike is fundamental to the success of this tactic.

The suspect makes a sudden movement as though to draw a knife, 436, or a hitting weapon, 437.

436. Draw and strike at the reaching hand or wrist and . . .

437. without hesitation grip his hand with your left hand as you move around behind him . . .

438. twisting the captured arm as you move. Strike into the shin or knee to weaken and distract, allowing you to put him onto his knees or onto the ground for handcuffing.

When using the baton at the knee level or lower, special care must be taken to avoid bending down into a vulnerable off-balance stance. Keep your head out of fist range. Maintain a good guard.

Greatest flexibility of response is available to you if you can use either kicking or baton blows, or if you can combine them as needed.

434

435

436

437

438

SOLO PRACTICE ROUTINE

Traditional Asian stick fighting methods often include formal
routines of movements which simulate striking blows. These
routines are intended to develop and maintain skill in handling
the weapon. Sometimes they are taught as though they could
be applied to practical self-defense. In my view, such routines
tend to inhibit flexible responses unless they are supplemented
with original work.

Following is an exercise developed by Officer Nickoloff. When
you can perform this routine smoothly and gracefully you should
proceed to the next step which is to invent your own routines.

This routine is shown practiced from a standstill--an excellent
procedure. Variations of this routine can be practiced moving--
advancing, retreating and turning in a circle.

439. Start from a ready position, well-balanced, facing forward.
The weapon is in the ring but held horizontally for quick draw.

440. The quick draw action is followed through into a backhand snap.

441. Without hesitation, a downward snap is executed.

442. An up-and-outward thrust is followed by a . . .

443. small-arc forehand blow.

439

440

441

442

443

444

445

446

444. The arc is reversed and a downward whipping action begins . . .

445. and is carried through and . . .

446. immediately reversed to strike upward. Maintain this guarded, ready position and repeat the routine advancing, retreating and turning.

PRACTICE PROCEDURES/FLEXIBILITY & QUICK RESPONSE

It is not necessary for officers to practice full contact stick-hitting blows on each other. In my view, a better method of practice is light, touching blows in beginning baton practice and, as skill develops, to simulate moderately forceful blows *without* making contact. This enhances control capability as it develops technical skill. Finally, officers should practice fully released blows, moderate blows and light blows against inanimate objects to test their ability to regulate the force of any blow. It is not only the ability to hit hard which is being practiced, it is the ability to deliver a moderate or light blow when such responses would be appropriate. You are learning to control yourself and your stick weapon.

447   448

447, 448. Your partner holds a target object as shown. Practice hitting two fast consecutive blows--to one side and then the other. Two methods of hitting are to hit a forceful snap blow, delivering as much power as you can but keeping the action within a very small, tight arc; and to hit a light or moderate blow, first on one side and then on the other. The arc of movement from the first side to the second should be very short. Wrist action is primary. The movement is similar to the cuts used in fencing.

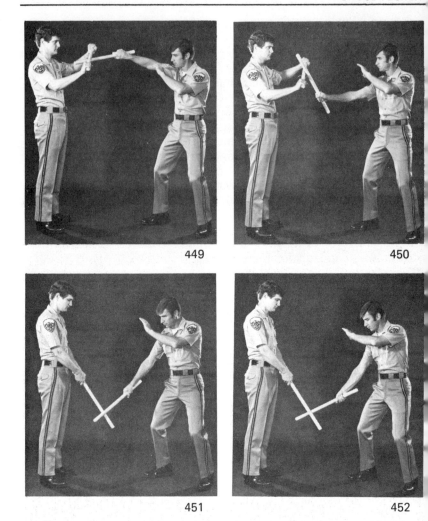

449   450

451   452

449, 450. Your partner holds the target with both hands; the hitting target is the center of the held stick. Follow the procedure as in 447 and 448 but use a snappy, short upward blow followed by a snappy downward cut. Movement is concentrated in the wrist. Practice forceful blows. Practice moderate and light blows.

451, 452. The target is held low. The practice procedure is like that in 447 and 448. Hit the target with two blows, first on one side and then on the other. The arc should be small. Emphasize wrist action. Practice light and forceful blows.

MOVING OBJECT PRACTICE PROCEDURE

To hit a person's moving arm or kicking leg requires some control and accuracy practice. The improvised training equipment shown here is safe to use and cheap to make. Foam rubber or flannel toweling taped around a dowel makes an excellent "arm" hitting target. A 1" dowel is a fairly sturdy training aid. If you break them when you do not intend to, you are hitting with greater force than is needed. You can hit with follow-through action and you can practice all of the hitting methods you have learned.

The partner who holds the padded stick should move it about in a way which most closely resembles hitting, punching and reaching actions.

A "leg" hitting target can be made of a broomstick or heavier dowel, well padded with foam rubber or toweling. Do not use pins to fasten the padding on either stick; use tape or adhesive.

453   454

453, 454. Using the arm stick as a target, practice hitting high and mid-area blows against the moving object.

455   456

455. Practice two-handed grip blows against the moving object.

456. Using the leg stick as a target, practice striking and blocking.
Maintain good balance and a guarded stance.

Because the techniques in this course have been selected for their
relative simplicity as well as for efficiency, it is not necessary to
engage in heavy programs of constant practice and training.
Occasional in-service review sessions are necessary for maintaining
functional skill. Because street application of any particular
technique is likely to be infrequent, practice from time to time
is the only way to maintain familiarity, dexterity and quick and
appropriate response.

Any physical activity which enhances your general health and
endurance will also enhance your ability to use defense and control tactics to protect yourself and work at a high level of professional competence.

457. Just a few of the many different batons widely used in different law enforcement agencies.

457

CHOOSING A STICK WEAPON

There is no general agreement about the type of baton which is best for police work. The extent of the lack of consensus can be measured by looking through equipment advertisements of the professional journals and by observing the wide range of stick weapons used in departments throughout the country and the world. The major variations are in the kinds of material used in sticks and in the different lengths--ranging from the six inch handstick to the staff-like riot weapons used in some areas. In recent years Asian styles of stick weapons adapted from ancient farm implements have been adopted and discarded as they proved less practical than standard batons.

The principle criteria for adopting a baton should be: Can the baton be used by officers who have had the amount of training which is ordinarily given in that department? And, does the baton suit the needs of the department? It is easier to change a baton than it is to retrain an entire department in an exotic style of stick work.

To determine the practicality of any stick under consideration for adoption, the stick and its deployment should be demon-strated by an officer who has had basic training in its use. Demon-stration by an expert does not allow proper evaluation of the baton. An expert stick fighter can use any kind of stick with im-pressive skill. How is the same stick going to be used by the average officer?

INDEX

BRUCE TEGNER books are on sale at bookstores and magazine stands throughout the world. If your local dealer does not stock the titles you want, you may order directly from the publisher. For free descriptive brochure, write to:

THOR PUBLISHING COMPANY
P.O. BOX 1782
VENTURA, CA 93001